TURNING DECORATIVE
BOWLS

TURNING DECORATIVE
BOWLS

RICHARD FINDLEY

Foreword

This book is a collection of bowl turning articles published in *Woodturning* magazine during my Editor's Challenge series. The concept of the series came about during a discussion with the late editor, Mark Baker. I had written numerous articles covering many aspects of turning and we were looking for something new when I suggested that he could set a challenge each month, whether that be to use a tool I'd never used, make something I'd never made before or to incorporate a material or technique that was new to me.

The readers were used to step-by-step articles explaining how to make a particular project, but those projects were always successful; this would be something new with a little added jeopardy that I might not actually be successful in completing a particular challenge. As a professional turner, part of my day-to-day work is to solve problems and work out the best way to complete a project, so I would be using some of my existing skill set to complete these challenges, but there would always be something to take me out of my comfort zone, to push my boundaries and to test my skills. The challenges also gave me the opportunity to 'play', something that I don't normally get to do as a full-time production turner. As such, this book is not a collection of how-to articles, more a series of stories of how I approached each challenge, dealt with issues that came up and how each was completed. Some were, of course, more successful than others but those that appear in this book are the ones I am most pleased with and many of the finished items have pride of place in my own home.

As the months went by, it became clear that readers were enjoying these new articles. I think they connected with readers in a way that other articles didn't because they could empathize with some of the problems I met along the way, they could problem-solve along with me, wonder how they would do it and follow the journey from start to finish. Many sent me pictures of their own projects that they had made, inspired by these challenges. Even some years after I finished writing these and moved on to a new series, people still commented how much they enjoyed the challenges.

I am grateful to Mark Baker for trusting me with these articles and would like to thank the small team at GMC for making writing them so easy and enjoyable. When the subject of making a book came up, we agreed that it would be a great opportunity to gather these articles together in one place and re-publish them so readers, both old and new, could enjoy them again and hopefully be inspired to try some new techniques as I was when the challenges were originally set.

Richard Findley

Contents

The basics of bowl turning

Tool manufacturers invest a large amount of time and money into research and development, and are always coming up with new and innovative tools to solve our woodturning problems – sometimes they even solve problems we didn't know we had! What then, would your reaction be if I told you I had a tool that could do more than 90% of bowl turning? It can do heavy roughing cuts, shaping cuts, fine finishing cuts, scraping and shear cutting. The best thing about this amazing tool is that, more than likely, you already own it, because it's a bowl gouge. In this chapter, I'll take you through the basics of choosing and using turning tools and demonstrate the essential cuts and techniques for turning a bowl.

WHICH BOWL GOUGE?

Bowl gouges come in various shapes and sizes. Some are recommended or even signed by professionals that use a certain profile or tool form. For the beginner, the choice can be completely overwhelming.

My first suggestion is to stick to one of the big name manufacturers. There are cheaper makes out there but, as with so many things, you get what you pay for.

The shape of the flute is the next thing to look at. There are three main flute shapes. One is based loosely around a 'V' shape, one is more 'U' shaped and the third is known as a parabolic flute. This is my own preferred flute shape and most of the best-known bowl turners around the world seem to agree, so if you are buying a new bowl gouge I would recommend a parabolic flute. However, the fact is, they all work and which you use or prefer will actually be down to which you buy first, because as you learn to handle a tool and manipulate it to make the cuts you want, you will learn to love the tool. You will most likely have the tool for several years, and by the time it wears down to an unusable length, it will feel almost like an extension of your arm.

Size is the other consideration. My preference is for a ⅜in (10mm) tool. I find this a very versatile size, which can produce a small 4in (100mm) nut bowl, a large 18in (450mm) platter or 13in (350mm) fruit bowl. The larger tools are useful for bigger or deeper bowls where the added weight and strength of the tool offers an easier or smoother cut by dampening vibration.

At this point it's worth pointing out that the sizing of bowl gouges varies depending upon which side of the Atlantic you are on. Here in the UK, bowl gouges are – confusingly – roughly measured across the width of the flute, so my preferred ⅜in (10mm) bowl gouge is made from ½in (12mm) steel, whereas in the US, the diameter of the tool steel is measured, as it is for spindle gouges, so it may be worth checking with your supplier before buying, just to make sure you are getting the size you think you are.

A selection of bowl gouges

Bowl gouge flute shapes

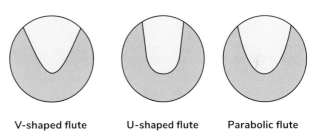

V-shaped flute   U-shaped flute   Parabolic flute

The range of flute shapes available

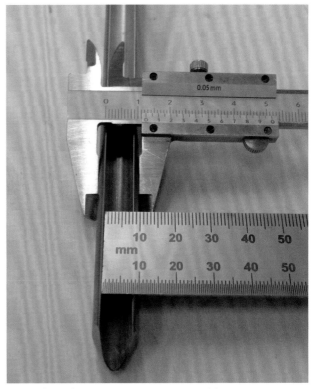

My ⅜in (10mm) bowl gouge showing its actual dimensions

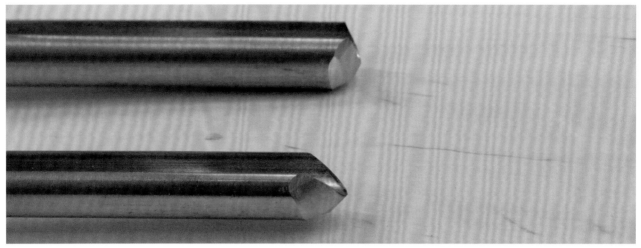

My preferred grinds of 50° on my main ⅜in (10mm) gouge and 65° on my ½in (12mm) bottoming bowl gouge

WHAT ANGLE AND WHAT GRIND?

Almost everyone you talk to will recommend a different grind shape and angle. Many people use two or more gouges with different profiles. My preferred grind works for 90% of the bowls I make; I also have a secondary gouge with a steeper angle for deeper or more enclosed shapes where accessing the base is difficult. I'm aware that I am just another one of those people suggesting grinds and angles, and what I recommend may not suit you. What I can say with confidence is that it works for me and many students I have taught, having tried my grind, have asked me to re-grind their tool to match.

I use an angle of around 50°, with a 'long grind', although my long grind is nowhere near as long as many people use. The angle is not that important, but I have found that 50° with the heel removed for clearance allows for cutting of most bowl shapes you will want to make. A steeper 65° tool with a more traditional profile reaches anything I can't with my main gouge.

The thing to look for when grinding is the shape of the wing that you produce, no matter the length – you are looking for a slightly convex curve to the wing when viewed from the side. If you are producing a concave curve, it will not work well. The reason for this concavity is that you have ground too much steel from the wings, so go gently on that grinder.

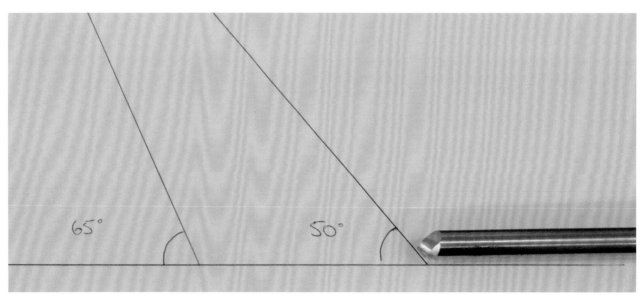

My low-tech method for checking the grind angle

PULL OR DRAW CUT

I usually do most of the roughing cuts and initial shaping of a bowl with a draw cut. It is best to initially start cutting near the tip of the tool. This produces a small and controllable shaving. When you feel confident with this, you can then adjust the presentation to allow more of the wing to engage in the cut. You will see that this produces a much wider shaving. Heavy and aggressive cuts are absolutely fine, as long as you are ready to make them. When a heavy cut happens and you aren't expecting it, it's known as a catch. So take your time and get to know the feel of the cuts and how best to present the tool. It is worth pointing out that the longer your grind, the bigger and more aggressive your cuts – and so potential catches – can be. Once you are happy and comfortable, you can begin to add shape to your bowl. With this cut, the flute remains at around 10 o'clock, and the cut comes off the left-hand section of the tip and wing of the tool, as shown in the pictures below. Throughout the cut, the tool should be tucked into your body and the movement comes from your body, rather than your arms and wrists.

I find the draw cut great for quickly and efficiently removing unwanted timber. It doesn't always leave the best finish, but that isn't a problem at this stage in a turning because the focus is on the shape.

Using the tip is a more controllable way of working until you feel comfortable

The flute of this gouge is at 12 o'clock and the arms of the clock show the positions of 10 and 2

Allowing more of the wing to cut is a more aggressive cut

The draw cut in action, quickly removing the waste material

FINISHING CUTS

There are two cuts that I use to produce a surface ready for sanding. The first option is a traditional push cut. With this the flute sits at around the 10 o'clock position and the cut comes from near the tip. The bevel needs to lightly rub – or more correctly, glide – behind the cut. To achieve this, the handle needs to start pointing out, usually across the lathe bed, and, as the cut is made and the shape of the bowl followed, the handle will come round towards your body and swing in an arc. The tip of the tool needs to be presented in the same position relative to the wood throughout the cut, so all of the handle movement – the sideways movement and the swing – is happening to enable this. Because the shape of the bowl has been formed with the draw cut it should now be as you planned, so the aim of this push cut is to remove a very small but even amount, all the way around the outside of the bowl, similar to peeling the skin from an orange, to reveal what is below. Aim to keep this cut small, maybe 1–2mm at most; go steady and smoothly to the top edge of the bowl.

With this cut, as with all cuts used in turning, moving smoothly is important. Every time you have to change stance, move your feet or hesitate, it will add a line, lump or bump into the surface of the bowl, so smooth is the key here. It takes practice, but when it all goes to plan, the finish and surface is superb.

What if it doesn't quite go to plan and there are bumps on the bowl? You could try a shear cut. With the same tool, all you have to do is change the presentation to produce a shear cut. By dropping the handle low and keeping it in against your body or top of the leg, and rotating the flute so it is almost facing the wood, you are presenting the lower edge of the tool – no bevel contact – to the wood at about a 45° angle. This is again a very light cut but the advantages are all about control. The tool is now tucked back in to your side, so the movement comes from your body rather than your arms. The other advantage is visibility. Because you are now standing in front of the bowl, you can see the shape of the bowl perfectly, and are able to focus on and adjust certain areas to produce that perfect shape and finish.

Because there is no bevel contact, there is no burnishing effect, so the surface is not shiny, but if you look at the shavings that you are producing, you can be sure the surface will be smooth and free from torn or pulled grain. If, during the cut, the shaving changes from a really fine wispy shaving to a thicker curl, it is usually because the presentation has changed from shearing to something closer to the draw cut, so stop and check your tool presentation.

The push cut in action

The tool position for a shear cut

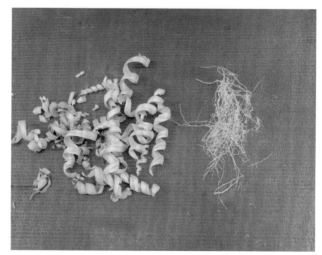
The sort of shaving you will produce: on the left is the draw cut, and on the right the finishing shear cut

INSIDE THE BOWL

With the outside sanded and the bowl reversed on the chuck, you are ready to work the inside. There are two main methods for removing the centre from a bowl. The first is the most traditional method.

Using the bowl gouge in a push cut, with the flute at around 2 o'clock, you start near the centre and take a small bowl-shaped cut. This is repeated time after time, becoming wider and deeper until you reach the rim of the bowl, then take a final finishing cut from the rim down to the bottom, in a single, smooth sweeping cut. There can be a problem with this, however. If your bowl has a fairly thin, even wall, or is large or perhaps made from unseasoned timber, by the time you have removed all of that wood from the centre, the bowl will probably have become a little – or sometimes a lot – oval, and will be vibrating and chattering against the tool, making that final smooth finishing cut virtually impossible to complete satisfactorily. Taking a single cut from top to bottom can also make it difficult to maintain an even wall thickness, so I use a slightly different technique here.

Starting at the edge or rim of the bowl, I work down in stages, focusing on perhaps an inch of depth at a time.

I make a series of scooping cuts down into the bowl, with the flute at 2 o'clock. When I run out of space to make more cuts, I rotate the gouge so the flute faces around 10 o'clock, and cut down a series of steps, which creates space to work while keeping a core in the wood to help with stability.

Once I have made enough space to work, I make a finishing push cut on this first section of the bowl with the flute at around 2 o'clock. Once I'm happy with the surface and the wall thickness I continue with the next stage. If the bowl decides to move now, I only have to sand, which is much easier on an uneven shape than trying to cut with a gouge.

The central cone-shaped bulk can be removed and gradually the inside of the bowl takes shape. Sometimes, most commonly on bowls with a tight curve, you can find that you are leaving rows of quite regular ridges in the surface. This is a problem caused by the bevel of your gouge. The best analogy for this is when cutting discs on a bandsaw. If you have a wide blade, you cannot cut a smooth continuous curve because the back of the blade binds in the cut. The answer is to use a narrower blade. This is exactly what is happening in the bowl. The heel

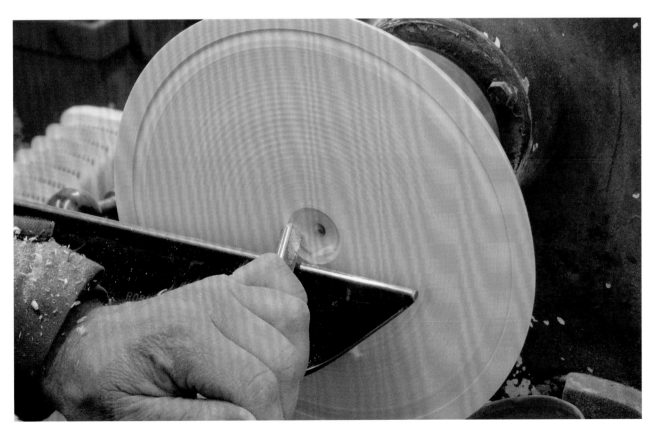

Starting the traditional hollowing cut from the centre

of the gouge is rubbing and preventing that perfectly smooth curve. By grinding away the heel you shorten the bevel and so allow it to cut the curve you are after.

If I'm turning a small, deep or enclosed bowl, sometimes the shaft of the tool can foul on the rim of the bowl. If this happens I switch to my ½in (12mm) 'bottoming bowl gouge' with the steeper 65° angle, which allows access to the bottom of this style of bowl with ease.

The final cuts can pose a few problems as a small pip or dimple in the bottom is easy to create. The key is to slow down the cut; the centre of the bowl is spinning much slower than the outer edge, so the tool's feed rate needs to be slower too. Keep the pressure even and the movement smooth, and the final little pip should just drop off into the flute of the gouge.

Starting the cut at the rim for the step method

Making space to continue hollowing

The final cut, removing the pip in the bottom of the bowl

SCRAPERS AND CHUCKING

Generally, I can do most of the turning on a bowl with a bowl gouge but there are two occasions when I will use a scraper on a bowl. The first is to cut the chucking tenon or recess. For bowl work I will almost always use a tenon rather than a recess purely because a tenon gives me excess wood that I can shape into a foot or remove completely if the design suits it better. Recesses will tend to lead to bowls with wide bottoms, which is fine if this is your plan, but if you want a delicate base, foot or even a round-bottomed bowl, there is no way a recess will work. Whichever you choose though, using a skew chisel as a scraper to form the dovetail shape works perfectly. It is important to know, or carefully measure, the perfect gripping size of your chuck so you can form your tenon or recess to achieve the best possible grip from the jaws; too big or too small and the jaws don't hold properly and so the bowl won't be securely held by the chuck.

SCRAPERS INSIDE THE BOWL

Occasionally, when finishing the inside of a bowl, I will have a small ripple or hump that I just can't seem to shift with a bowl gouge so I might turn to a scraper for help. I use negative rake scrapers, which have a bevel top and bottom and use a burr to cut. I use 35° for both bevels, but there are a lot of different opinions out there on this subject. A curved negative rake scraper is ideal for those tricky spots on the inside of a bowl that are causing problems. Scrapers tend to work best on side grain (like at the bottom of a bowl) or end grain (when hollowing an end grain box) but they don't handle the constant change of end grain to side grain that you find on the side of a bowl, so on the inside of a bowl I would only use them across the bottom and somewhat up the curve of the wall but I would avoid working too far up the side wall as this often leads to torn grain. A light touch and a fresh burr will leave a smooth surface ready for sanding.

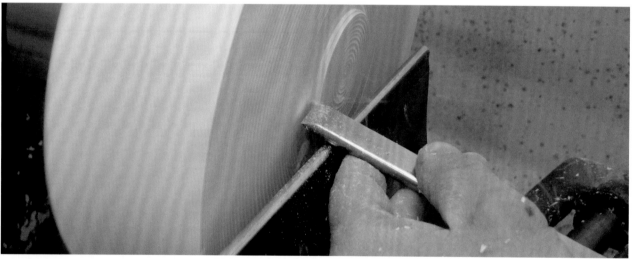

Scraping the chucking tenon with my skew

Using a scraper on the inside of a bowl

REVERSE CHUCKING

To leave a professional finish on the base of my bowls I like to reverse chuck them and remove or rework the tenon. There are a number of ways to do this including vacuum chucking and specialist 'Cole' jaws but I like to use a very simple and inexpensive method. I have a disc of MDF fixed to a faceplate and I simply bring up the tailstock and sandwich the bowl between the disc and the live centre. I can then turn the base down to a small pip that is easily carved and power sanded away to leave a perfectly finished base to the bowl. I used to pad the MDF with paper towel or router matting but all of these can leave marks on the rim of the bowl so now I just place the bowl against the MDF.

Reverse chucking the bowl

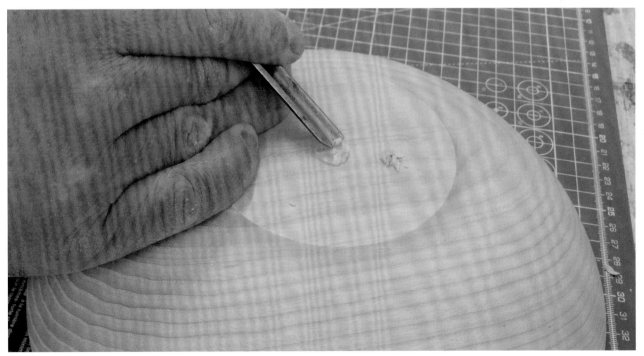
Removing the remaining pip with a carving gouge

Segmented bowl

Making this bowl was my first attempt at segmenting – I had always dismissed it in the past as being a rather fiddly technique, having to stick little bits of wood together to make a bowl. I wasn't sure whether this challenge would convert me, but I was looking forward to trying it out. I decided to start with the simplest project I could think of: a bowl made from solid timber, with a segmented ring fitted for decorative interest. Many segmented bowls are completely segmented, from base to rim, but I figured that a couple of rings shouldn't be too difficult and would give me a taste of the technique.

RESEARCH

I have many books that show how to form a segmented ring. In theory, it should simply be a case of working out how many sections I would like, working out the angle needed, cutting it accurately and gluing the sections together. The ring, once dry, can then be sandwiched into a block of timber and turned, almost as a normal bowl. I wasn't sure it would be quite that simple in practice, so before I began work, I did a little more research.

I knew there are a number of different ways of cutting the segments, so I needed to decide which would be best for me. I have seen people use a mitre saw (sometimes known by the catchy name of a 'sliding compound mitre saw' or SCMS for short); some use a disc sander; while others use a saw bench (or tablesaw).

My workshop is set up so that I can do all kinds of woodwork. I own all three of these machines, but my SCMS was quite inexpensive, bought with the intention of easily cross-cutting lengths of timber, and isn't terribly accurate. From my experience in joinery workshops, it seems that you need to spend some serious money to get an SCMS that would be consistently accurate enough for this kind of work. My disc sander is, to be honest, a little unloved and abused. It isn't used a great deal, so the sanding disc is rather past its best, which immediately ruled this out for the job in hand. My tablesaw, on the other hand, is used almost daily. It is accurate and has sharp blades, so it was the obvious choice.

I felt that using a jig would give me the best results. My search for a suitable jig began on YouTube, where I found a video of a jig that made sense to me and would be easy to construct.

THE MATHS OF SEGMENTING

It became clear that I needed to do some maths to work out some of the details. Maths was never really a strong point for me at school. While I had a grasp of the basics and enough to see me through, the subject never really held me. I think this was mostly because it seemed so irrelevant to real life. Once I left school to work for my Dad, I learned maths in a more practical way. We used to make fittings for bay windows, so I became quite familiar with working with angles and how to manipulate them to my advantage. That should be a useful skill here.

My main problem was that I couldn't quite remember some of the intricacies of the maths required for this job. Thankfully we now have the internet to hand at the touch

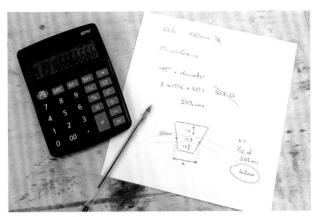
My rough workings

The segment used for this bowl

of a phone screen, so the equations were easy to find. My first decision was how many segments I should use to form the ring. I could literally use any number here, but to help me visualize it, I decided to go with 12, so it could be divided up the same as a clock face. I find being able to visualize things very important, so using this familiar pattern made sense. Based on the ring being 12 segments I could work out the angles:

A circle has 360°
360 ÷ 12 = 30°

However, when cutting a mitre joint, as I would be when segmenting, each side of the mitre is half of this angle, so each segment needs an angle of 15° on each side. Next, I had to calculate the circumference of my bowl blank, so I would know how big to make my ring. The diameter of the blank is 6¼in (160mm).

Circumference = π x diameter
π (Pi) = 3.141592
Diameter = 6¼in (160mm)
Circumference = 3.141592 x 6.5 (160) = 19¾in (503mm)

So the circumference will be roughly 19¾in (503mm). At this stage, it seemed like a good idea to make the disc larger than the diameter of the bowl blank, so my plan was to make the segments around three times wider than my intended bowl thickness. This should give me plenty of leeway when gluing up. Erring on the side of caution, I calculated that ½in (12mm) should be more than thick enough for the wall thickness of the bowl, so 1½in (36mm)-wide segments would allow around ½in (12mm) either side of the bowl thickness. I made a simple sketch to show me the size I need for my segments.

MAKING THE JIG

The jig shown on YouTube was fully adjustable, but as I only intended to make this particular bowl with 15° mitres, I saw no need to go to the extra effort of doing the same with my jig. The design of the jig was simple enough. I started by cutting a strip of beech to run in the channel on the bed of the saw and fitted this to a piece of ²³⁄₃₂in (18mm) MDF, using glue and screws. I positioned the MDF so that it was oversized and, once fitted with the strip of beech, I could push it past the saw to give an accurate edge parallel to the saw blade. I could then use this edge to set my angles.

When fitting wooden battens to an MDF base board, a combination of glue and screws will give the strongest and longest-lasting combination of fixings. Often, however, as you drive in the screws, they can pull the batten away from the desired position. A useful tip to avoid this is to glue the batten and use a nail gun to grip it firmly in place, while you pilot drill and drive in the screws.

The first step for most jigs like this is to insert the beech strip in the slot on the saw bed

Using a pin gun to hold the batten in place before permanent fixing

Fixing the battens in place with glue and screws

Trimming a parallel edge to the base board

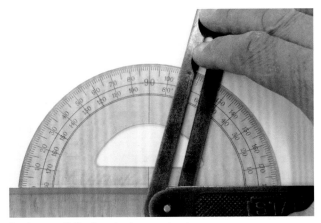
Setting my sliding bevel using a protractor

Fixing the battens to the base board, guided by the sliding bevel

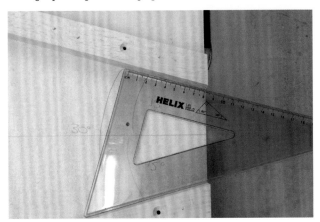

Checking the angles with a setting out triangle

My test cut is promising

SETTING UP THE JIG

I carefully set my sliding bevel to 15° and, using the cut edge of the MDF base board, positioned the battens and fixed them down. In the YouTube video, the guy uses a setting out triangle, which has 30°, 60° and 90° corners, to check the battens are set correctly. I did the same and was pleased that my original setting out was good.

You will notice that there are two battens fixed to the base board. I believe this is to minimize – or hopefully eradicate – problems with the angles. I tried using the standard mitre fence for my saw and simply turning the piece of wood over to alternate the angle on each block, but found it quite inaccurate. The problem was that, because the angle was repeated so many times around the ring, the fault was multiplied at every angle; for example, if you were even 1° out, by the time you get all the way round, you will be 24° out. By using this jig, with two battens that are a known 30° – thanks to the plastic triangle – the angles became far more accurate. Using some offcuts, I formed a ring using my mitre fence and one using the jig and the results speak for themselves. There was a tiny discrepancy, but I could

deal with this. At this point I realized that, had I made the jig adjustable, I would have been able to adjust the fault away. This experience could go in my ever-growing 'lessons learned' file!

EXPERIMENTING WITH GLUE-UPS

Now able to form the ring with some accuracy, I needed to find a way to glue the blocks together (I had ordered some Jubilee clips but they weren't large enough). A method I learned from my joinery experience is a rub joint.

By applying an even coat of glue to a surface, then rubbing two pieces of properly prepared timber together, air is squeezed out forming a kind of vacuum, which forms enough pressure to hold the two pieces of wood together while the glue dries. This is something that I knew the principle of, but again, had never used in angles, so I experimented on some of my trial cuts. I was amazed at the strength of the joint, especially as end grain to end grain joints are notoriously weak. Satisfied that this method would work, I set about cutting my segments and getting ready for the first glue-up.

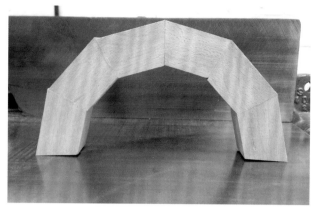

Run out on the first semicircle

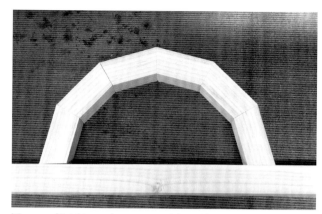

My second trial is much more promising using my jig

Preparing the timber with my planer-thicknesser

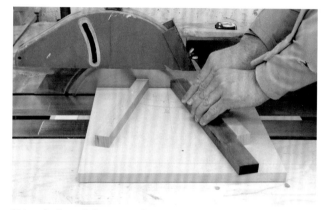

Using the jig and alternating between the two positions ...

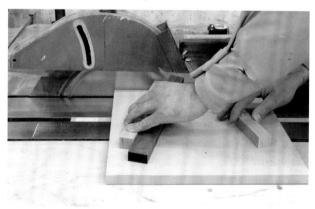

... to produce the correct angles on each segment

The semicircle laid out dry shows only a tiny discrepancy

The glue is spread with my finger

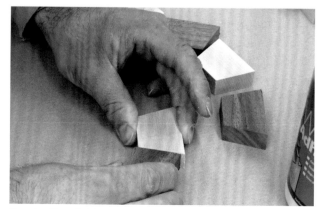

Forming the rub joint

GLUING THE SEGMENTS

I prepared pieces of American black walnut and maple using my planer-thicknesser to smooth and square up strips of material before cutting them into segments with the jig on the saw. I used a sharp, 96-tooth saw blade which cut very cleanly and then removed any wispy bits by rubbing them away with my fingernail. I laid out a sheet of brown craft paper on a flat area of my bench and gathered the segments together, alternating the walnut and maple to form a chequered pattern.

Using my finger, I spread an even smear of glue over one face and, laying the blocks flat on the bench, I rubbed the joint together. As I did this, I could feel the joint getting tighter, which was reassuring. I made sure the joint was flat and sitting evenly, then repeated the process. As my earlier experiment had shown a tiny discrepancy, I decided not to try to form a complete ring, but to form four half rings, which could be adjusted once dry and then glued up.

TYPES OF GLUE

In my workshop, I use two types of glue: polyurethane (PU) and resin-based, white wood glue. PU is great for big glue-ups or things that need to be done quickly, as it is incredibly strong, dries very quickly and is easy to apply. I use it in cartridge form, held in a sealant gun. The downside to PU is that it foams as it dries, which means you get great coverage, but it also requires good clamping pressure to keep all parts together, which I didn't have with this project.

The resin-based white glue, which I used here, is like a standard PVA. The beauty of this glue is that it forms a very strong bond with an almost invisible glue line and, most importantly of all, it resists creep. Creep is when the wood moves after it has been worked, which frustratingly means you can feel the join a short while after finishing the job; this is something I really want to avoid.

FLATTENING

With the semicircles left overnight to dry, I could look at forming the rings. Before anything else, I wanted to smooth the surfaces to ensure they were totally flat. I fixed a sheet of 180-grit abrasive tightly to a piece of MDF and carefully rubbed the semicircles over the abrasive. I kept it moving so I didn't wear down any one spot. As the abrasive was tightly wrapped around the MDF and was laying flat, it wouldn't round the edges of the timber. Regular checks ensured that I only did what was needed; no more and no less. I was pleased with how well this worked and I repeated the process at various stages of making the rings.

Flattening the rings

CORRECTING THE ANGLES

With the semicircles flattened, I needed a way to correct the angles, so another jig was in order. I had been mulling this over since realizing there was a slight correction needed and had come up with a simple jig that should do the job.

I repeated the first steps of the previous jig by cutting a batten for the slot in the saw and fixing it to a piece of $^{23}/_{32}$in (18mm) MDF, then running it past the saw to give a reference face, parallel to the saw blade. I fixed a toggle clamp onto the base board, fixed to a block to raise it to the correct position to hold the work. I then positioned my segmented semicircles right up against my reference edge, with just the tiniest piece overhanging the edge, which was removed, and corrected the angle. To ensure I held the semicircle firmly, without applying undue strain to the joints, I laid another piece of thinner $^{11}/_{32}$in (9mm) MDF over the segments to spread the gripping load. The jig simply slid past the blade and cut the edges of the segments, flush to the edge of the MDF. I tested it out first on my trial glue-up and was happy to proceed without any

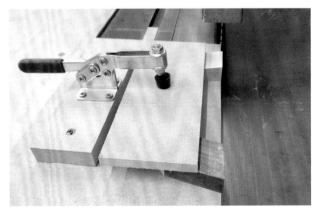
The correction jig set up to improve angles

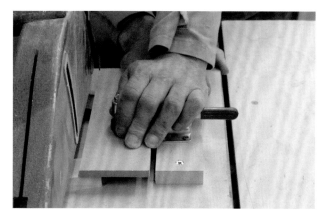

The correction jig in action

adjustment on my chequered segments. I could then glue the semicircles together to form my rings, using the same rub-joint technique as before.

SEGMENTED RINGS

After leaving them to dry overnight, I had my two rings. As before, I rubbed the new joints over the abrasive fixed to the MDF block to flatten them. They were now ready for the next stage of the glue-up: gluing the rings together. My next decision was whether to glue them like a chequerboard, with the maple directly over the walnut blocks, or to glue them like a brick wall, with the joint over the centre of the block beneath it. I decided to go with the chequerboard look, deciding that the brickwork design was probably best for bowls that are entirely segmented. As I only had two rings of segments, and was using timber that naturally lends itself to a chequerboard look, the choice was simple.

I spread an even layer of glue over one surface and rubbed the two rings together. I know that larger items

can slide while left unattended, so I pre-prepared some G-clamps and lightly gripped the rings in the correct position; I didn't want to damage any of the joints I had already formed, so I only used enough pressure to hold them in position while the glue cured.

MAKING THE BOWL

While the rings were drying, I prepared my bowl blanks; I used some 3⅛in (80mm) European oak that I had in stock. I planned to use a full thickness piece as the base, then fix the rings, adding another piece of oak to the top to form the rim. I cut a section long enough to get two blanks from and passed it over my planer to give a flat surface suitable for gluing the segmented rings to. I then deep cut it on the bandsaw to around 2in (50mm) deep, before cutting it into discs. This was deeper than I wanted the rim to be, but it's always better to have too much timber, rather than not enough. I fitted the two pieces together to see how they look best, with regards to the flow of the grain, and marked them with a pencil to guide me in the next part of the glue-up.

With the segmented rings dry and flattened again to ensure they were totally flat and ready for the final glue-up, I started to prepare everything I would need. This glue-up would definitely need clamps, so I used three large sash clamps. I always find glue-ups slightly stressful, but if they are well planned, things will usually go smoothly. It wasn't until I spread the glue and was trying to position the three sections together that I realized I had made an error. During the early stages, it seemed like a great idea to make the segmented rings bigger than the bowl blank to allow for positioning during glue-up, but now, in the midst of that glue-up, I realized that everything would be a lot easier if it was all the

The rub-joint to form the full ring

Spreading the glue to join the rings

same diameter. It was too late now, but in future, I know that the rings only need to be a tiny bit bigger than the bowl blank and not ½in (12mm) all around. After much wiggling and persuasion, the blocks were fixed in the sash clamps and all I could do was wait.

TURNING THE BOWL

The waiting time allowed me to mull over my error and think of ways to limit any problems. It occurred to me that the main focus of centring the blank on the lathe needs to be getting the segmented rings centralized. If they are off-centre, the segments on one side of the bowl will be larger than on the other. I'm not sure if this would be noticeable, but it could potentially be a problem.

To ensure the rings run centrally, I used a compass with the pencil well extended to find the centres of the bowl blanks, relative to the segmented rings rather than the actual centres of the oak blanks. I then mounted the block between centres to ensure it was positioned correctly. Using this method, I could adjust things as necessary, rather than having everything fixed in one position as it would be by a screw chuck or faceplate. Once I was happy that the rings were running centrally, I simply trued up the block with my bowl gouge, cut a holding spigot in what would be the top of the bowl and, holding the bowl with this spigot in the chuck, I turned the bowl as I normally would. The bowl was then sanded to 400 grit and finished with hard wax oil.

CONCLUSION

This bowl challenged me in a number of ways and enabled me to employ some of my joinery skills that have been underused in recent years. Were I to do this again, I would spend a little longer on the angle jig, although it worked admirably. I would also know to cut the rings to the same diameter as the bowl blanks to make the final glue-up easier.

Overall, I was very pleased with the end result. The joints are tight and there are only a couple where the joins of the chequering don't quite line up as well as I'd like, but I suspect this is due to me needing to adjust the semicircles to make them meet up properly. I'm certain that my next one will be better, if there is a next time!

I would recommend this project to anyone who feels they have mastered turning standard bowls and wants a challenge to further their woodworking and turning skills. This technique is a fascinating combination of skills that all need to be done to a high level to achieve an end result of good quality.

The final glue-up

The blank held between centres to centre the rings

Truing the blank

Open-segmented bowl

This challenge built upon the techniques I had learned with the segmented bowl (see pages 20–27). Open segmenting is when there are gaps between each segment, which gives additional visual impact to the work and, when combined with a pattern in the selected timbers, can be very impressive. As with many of these challenges, the open-segmenting technique was new to me and this project was sure to push my skills.

RESEARCH – JIG

I had previously made several items which involved either totally segmenting or partially segmenting, which gave me a good foundation for this piece. However, making a segmented piece full of gaps was still going to be quite a challenge. The first problem I needed to solve was exactly how to form the regular spacing involved in open segmenting. The answer was some sort of jig. I found plans for making jigs online but I decided to buy a ready-made, tried-and-tested jig – experience had already shown me how accurate everything needs to be in segmenting and I was also short on time – I didn't have several days to make, perfect and remake jigs.

During my research, I found several jigs available in the US. In the UK, segmented turner Sue Harker also makes versions of these jigs – known as segmenting wheels – and sells them through her website (www.sueharker.com) at a very reasonable price. There are also many other jigs and template guides for people to choose from.

Sue's jigs come in 6-, 12- and 18-segment variations, depending on the size of the item being made. The advice on the website led me to order the 18-segment wheel. The wheel itself is a fairly straightforward disc of MDF with securely fixed hardwood strips radiating out from the centre and was supplied with an instruction sheet which told me that I need to cut my segments with a 10° angle, along with a few other helpful pointers.

RESEARCH – DESIGN

My next step was to work out exactly what design of bowl I wanted to make. As I have realized in the past, the scope of my design is only limited by my imagination, skill level and lathe size. The segmenting wheel allows a bowl of up to about 9½in (240mm) to be made. For inspiration I searched online for bowls of various sorts, as well as segmented and open-segmented bowls. I was presented with a huge variety, ranging from poor in both design and execution to some really outstanding work with mind-bending patterns laid out in the segment positioning.

A couple caught my eye and planted the seed of an idea of creating a stepped pattern around the piece to give an interesting spiral pattern. Several pictures came up in my search based on the same idea so my mind was made up: I would make a simple open bowl and try to achieve a spiralling pattern running up the sides. I decided on a maple/walnut combination, with maple as the primary wood and walnut at the top and bottom and forming the spiral pattern.

Segmenting wheel jig with the first ring of segments in place

15mm (¹⁹⁄₃₂in) Thick segments
18 Segment open rings
Each ring has 12 x maple
6 x walnut

220mm (8³⁄₄in) Ø	Closed walnut segmented ring
210mm (8¹⁄₄in) Ø	32mm (1¹⁄₄in) segments
200mm (8in) Ø	30mm (1¹⁄₈in) segments
190mm (7½in) Ø	28mm (1¹⁄₈in) segments
180mm (7in) Ø	26mm (1¹⁄₁₆in) segments
170mm (6³⁄₄in) Ø	24mm (¹⁵⁄₁₆in) segments
160mm (6⁵⁄₁₆in) Ø	21mm (¹³⁄₁₆in) segments
130mm (5¹⁄₈in) Ø	18mm (²³⁄₃₂in) segments
110mm (4³⁄₈in) Ø	Solid walnut base

My plan for the open-segmented bowl

PLANNING

Woodturners aren't generally known as planners, but there was no way I would be able to pull this off without some sort of plan, so I drew out the bowl in full.

I decided to use ⅝in (15mm)-thick blocks. I thought an odd number of layers would look best, so I opted for seven rings, with a solid walnut base and a walnut segmented ring for the top.

A couple of simple calculations told me that 18 segments in the ring divides into 3, 6 times, so if every third block I added to the wheel was walnut, I would begin to achieve my intended pattern. This meant that on each ring of 18 segments, I would need 6 walnut and 12 maple.

Measuring and marking the diameters of each ring on the wheel

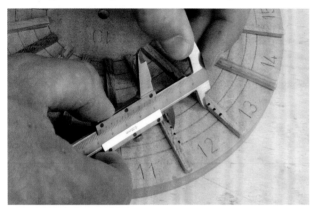
Measuring the size of each segment

Setting the mitre fence to 10°

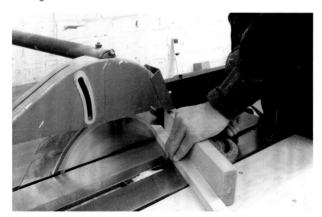
Cutting the segments

TIMBER PREPARATION

To begin, I fed the strips of maple and walnut through my thicknesser to take them down to the ⅝in (15mm).

Unlike a closed segmented job, I couldn't simply work out the circumference and divide it by the number of segments to find out the size of each – I needed to bring the segmenting wheel into play. I took the diameters of each ring from my full-sized drawing and marked them on the wheel.

From these marks I was able to measure the width of each segment and then add this information to my drawing. I could then begin cutting the blocks; I set the mitre fence on the sawbench to 10° using my digital protractor, so I could safely cross cut and begin cutting blocks.

BEGINNING THE GLUE-UP

I cut a disc of 2in (50mm)-thick walnut, turned it to 4¼in (110mm) diameter and cut a tenon into the underside, which would make mounting my glue-up in the chuck easier when the time came.

Before doing any gluing, I needed to decide how I would clamp the layers of segments together. I looked around the workshop for something heavy. I picked up the cast-iron centre steady that came with my Wadkin lathe and a couple of pieces of hardwood. Altogether, they weighed nearly 55lb (25kg), which I figured would be enough – generally the more pressure the better.

The segments in the first ring were all ¹¹⁄₁₆in (18mm) long and slotted into the wheel as planned. I added a small blob of glue to the centre of each segment and placed the walnut disc centrally on top. I then added my weights and left it to dry.

After about an hour I gently removed the weights and jig. A light tap with a mallet on the jig easily released the jig from the glue-up. The first ring seemed to be holding well. I added the next ring of segments, which were ¹³⁄₁₆in (21mm) long, to the wheel. This time I carefully added two lines of glue to the segments, avoiding the centre which will line up with the gap in the previous layer. In my research only one article that I read mentioned cleaning excess glue with pipe cleaners. I thought this would be quite a labour-intensive job, so better to avoid getting glue there in the first place. Importantly, the glue I used dries clear, so any tiny amounts of squeeze-out would be invisible once fully cured.

I carefully placed the base of the bowl on to the next ring of segments in the wheel, lining up the gaps with the centre of the segment above it, held it in place for a few moments while the glue adhered and added the weights.

Gluing the walnut base to the first ring of segments

Heavy weights used to clamp the glue-up together

The base and first ring released from the wheel

TO FLATTEN OR NOT?

I read several articles on the subject before I began this project and one process mentioned is to flatten each row of segments before moving on to the next. I decided against it for two reasons. First, the authors of the articles in question were using the lathe to glue up the segments, making it very easy to sand each row flat before moving on to the next. Second, I was working to a limited time frame and flattening each ring would entail leaving the glue to fully cure before moving on to the next, meaning making only one, perhaps two, rings a day at most.

I decided to proceed without flattening each ring; I knew it would not be a problem as long as the wood was properly prepared and I applied good, even pressure while the glue grabbed. With this method I could carefully add a ring about every hour and get all of the open segments glued together in a day.

Careful glue placement for the next open ring

Briefly holding the bowl in place while the glue grabs before adding weights

THE PATTERN

My pattern was formed of a slight spiral of walnut running up (or down, depending on your point of view) the side of the bowl. There would be six spirals, meaning it would be visible no matter what angle you view the bowl from. To achieve this, I placed a block of walnut in every third space on the segmenting wheel. When I placed the bowl on top of the blocks in the wheel, I just needed to make sure I rotated the pattern by one place each time, so the walnut blocks were diagonal to each other.

The spiral pattern on the inside of the bowl before turning

WALNUT SEGMENTED RING

While the open segments were drying, I could work on the closed-segmented ring of walnut for the top. Previously the most segments I had put into a ring was 12, but the same principle applies to an 18-segment ring, the difference being the angle on each segment is now 10°. I chose 18 as it allowed me to place the joins over the centre of each of the 18 segments in the top ring of the bowl, continuing the brickwork pattern of gluing up, which should provide the very strongest end result.

I worked out the circumference of the ring I needed to make and divided it into 18. Rounding up to the nearest full number, I cut the segments to 1½in (39mm) long. I then rub-jointed semicircles of nine segments each together and left them to dry while I worked on the rest of the bowl.

After a couple of hours, I very carefully flattened them enough to place on my jig to level the unglued faces so they met up perfectly. I then rub-jointed the semicircles into a full ring and left them overnight to fully dry.

Once they were fully cured I could fully flatten both faces of the walnut ring in preparation to adding it to the bowl.

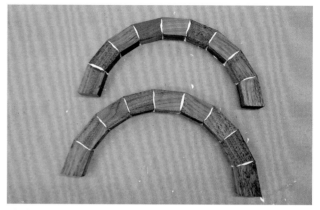

The beginnings of the walnut ring

Truing up the joining faces of the two semicircles

The ring set aside to dry

Flattening before final glue-up

I rubbed it repeatedly over a piece of 180-grit abrasive wrapped tightly around a board of MDF, regularly turning it to ensure it remained flat. Once I was satisfied that it was totally flat, I cleaned off all the dust and got ready for the last stage of the glue-up.

FINAL GLUE-UP

After gluing the seven layers of open segmenting I was well practised at it, only this time I added the glue to the centre of each of the top rings of open segments, avoiding the glue spreading into the openings.

I placed a piece of flat hardwood on the floor to give a solid base on which to sit the bowl and load the weights. I added the glued bowl, carefully lining up the joints with the centre of each of the top segments, held it for a moment to allow the glue to lightly grab, and then added the hardwood blocks and centre steady, along with a few other heavy things I could easily get my hands on, and left it overnight to fully dry before I could begin turning.

Careful glue placement ready for the walnut ring

Final glue-up under weights

TURNING

Looking at the bowl blank, it was hard to know if the glue-up had been entirely successful, but it looked promising and the spiral pattern had gone to plan. I placed the bowl in the chuck, using the chucking spigot I turned at the beginning, and made a start on turning the outside. I used a ½in (13mm) bowl gouge (⅝in/16mm bar) to turn the outer shape. It cut cleanly and I quickly formed a flowing curve. One concern I had was that the segments would chip out into the openings, with them being unsupported by the next block, but as none of the articles I had read mentioned this as a potential issue I carried on as normal, checking regularly and was pleased to find there was no breakout. Once the shape was cut without any steps still showing, I switched to a shear cut, using the wing of the gouge, and produced a beautifully smooth and clean surface which I carefully hand sanded from 180 to 400 grit.

Examining the outside, I was pleased with the quality of the joins. There didn't appear to be any significant gaps (apart from those that were supposed to be there), so I decided to continue with the inside of the bowl. If I had been nervous in any way I could have wrapped the outside in clingfilm, which is a technique often employed by hollow-form turners working with wood with natural faults, such as knots, cracks and voids.

I began turning the inside with the same bowl gouge but found the tool bounced too much on the uneven surface. I tried a carbide probe tool, which worked much better. With this tool I completely smoothed out the walls of the bowl but struggled to achieve a perfect curve, so I went back to the bowl gouge and took a couple of bevel-rubbing push cuts down the walls, which achieved the desired result.

As I turn, I often touch the work to feel the progress of a curve, but in this instance I was careful to stop the lathe when I felt for the curve. The surface wasn't sharp but, because of the gaps, it didn't feel smooth and it was hard to judge in the normal way.

The bowl was reasonably deep so my usual 50° bowl gouge cut all down the side wall. However, I swapped to an 65° gouge which allowed better access around the bottom corner and across the base. As I had on the outside, I carefully hand sanded from 180 to 400 grit. I took great care to keep the abrasive trailing as it could be snatched from my hand if it caught in the openings between the segments.

All glued up and ready to turn

Turning the outside

The outside curve is coming along well and showing no signs of break-out

Shear cutting the outside

Using the carbide probe to smooth the inside

Reverse turning the base

FINISHING THE BASE

The walnut block for the base was thicker than it needed to be, which allowed good access while I was turning, but I now needed to finish it to suit the rest of the bowl. I have a disc of MDF permanently attached to a faceplate which I use for remounting bowls. I brought up the tailstock and sandwiched it between the disc and the live centre, which gave me good access to turn the base down to a small nub, which I carved away with a carving gouge and then power sanded the base to 400 grit.

Spraying acrylic lacquer finish

FINISHING

I was a little concerned about finishing the bowl. Most of the articles I read suggested spray finishing, as this gets between the openings best without having to individually paint each one with a tiny brush. I used satin acrylic lacquer, which worked perfectly. Before the last coat I lightly rubbed the bowl back with a fine abrasive pad to give a totally smooth finish.

CONCLUSION

I enjoyed this open-segmented project far more than I thought I would. The prospect of gluing little blocks together to make bigger projects had never really appealed to me before, but once I passed a couple of hurdles regarding accuracy and realized the scope of design possibilities, I felt like I might even do more in the future. The result may be far from perfect but the process has given me a really good understanding of the techniques involved and I feel I can only improve from here. I think the base of this bowl could have been smaller, which would have improved the curve further. But overall, I am pleased with the outcome.

Staved bowl

This project, a staved bowl made from two contrasting timbers, uses some advanced turning techniques. In a previous challenge for the magazine, I had made a staved barrel box, but this bowl would be taking things a step further. The bowl's sides will need to taper out to allow me to turn some shape into it. Tapers and mitres combined are challenging, because it means forming what is known as a compound angle, which slopes in two directions at once. I didn't have much experience with compound angles but the experience I did have told me I was going to be scratching my head over this one.

RESEARCH

With a picture in mind of what I wanted to make but only a vague idea as to how to do it, I set about doing some research. I asked a friend who has done some similar work for advice – sometimes there really is no point in struggling to work something out from scratch when there are more experienced people willing to point you in the right direction.

My friend sent me a few videos, which were a great help but also confirmed my worst fears that working out the compound angles would be a task for a mathematician.

Thankfully, I was also sent this link, woodgears.ca/ miter/splayed_miters.pdf, which includes a chart of the information needed to see clearly the angles required to form numerous tapered polygons – the proper name for the shaped blank I was going to make. This also explained very clearly why the angles change as the side angle or taper angle of the bowl changes.

As well as watching the videos, I bought a book on segmented turning by well-known segmented turner Malcolm Tibbetts, which came highly recommended. I also watched a number of other videos on the subject. One thing that struck me was that the most common way of forming the compound angles for each stave is to use a tablesaw with a tilting blade. I have an industrial quality saw but the blade is fixed, meaning I can use it to cut the angle of the stave but not the mitre.

Looking around my workshop, I had a new sliding compound mitre saw which, as the name suggests, is capable of producing the sort of angle I needed, but when I imagined the size and shape of each segment I was likely to need it made my fingers tingle so I decided against it for this project. I couldn't use my planer as

each segment would be too short to safely push over the cutter. I had a small disc sander, which I know many segmenters use, but I couldn't imagine being able to hold each piece successfully against the spinning abrasive disc, so discounted this too. After a little more thought I settled on a hybrid solution of cutting the triangular staves on a jig on the tablesaw and forming the mitre with a sharp hand plane.

DESIGN

Using the information from the online chart, I made a rough sketch of the bowl design – a simple curving bowl from a relatively small base flowing up to a rim of around 8in (200mm). I decided to work with 12 segments. Placing my protractor on the drawing showed a blank with its sides splayed at round 35° would work well. Using the chart, I worked out the following information: a bowl with a diameter of 8in (200mm) needs segments with a widest measurement of 2in (54mm). To achieve the wall angle of 35° on a 12-sided shape, each segment needs to be tapered to 12.24° and have a mitre of 8.74°. Thankfully, this was easy to work out from the chart, without any need to dust off my scientific calculator.

THE JIG

My next step was to make a jig for my saw to help me produce the triangles. Nearly all of the videos and articles I'd seen show the use of some sort of cradle that slides in the slot on the table of the saw, some more elaborate than others. Running a few ideas through my head, I decided simple was the best route to take. The sliding mitre fence on my saw is rock solid when it's locked, so I decided to take advantage of this. If it was less stable in use I would have built something separate.

Using some $^{11}/_{16}$in (18mm) MDF, I made a simple L-shaped board by screwing two pieces together.

The MDF jig

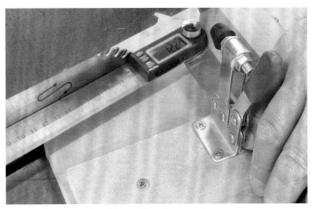

Setting the cut angle with my digital protractor

This formed a false sacrificial bed and a square back board against which I could rest the wood being cut. I screwed a toggle clamp to the base board to securely hold the wood in place, keeping my fingers away from the saw blade. The MDF jig was then clamped to the mitre fence to securely hold it in place.

I used my digital protractor, set to 12.25° (which is as close to 12.24° as I could get) to set the whole jig at the correct angle. Using a freshly sharpened, fine-tooth saw blade, I made a few practice cuts.

Satisfied with the results of these, I prepared some timber. Searching through my wood pile, I came across some sycamore and sapele in ideal sizes. The white of the sycamore should sit well next to the red/brown of the sapele. Using my planer-thicknesser I prepared blanks to 1⅛in (30mm) thick and around 2½in (60mm) wide, then cut them to 4¼in (110mm) lengths on the mitre saw (SCMS).

CUTTING THE TRIANGLES

The MDF fence was set up to use the end grain part of each piece of wood as the reference side. The wood sat firmly against the vertical part of the fence, was locked down using the toggle clamp and the first cut was made on each of the 12 pieces.

To form the second cut, I carefully measured the required 2in (54mm), marking it with a sharp pencil, and placed this mark against the edge of the MDF jig. As the edge of the jig was formed by the saw blade cutting in this position, I knew that by lining up my cut line here, I could achieve the desired result. Again, I locked the wood in place with the toggle clamp and made the cut. So far, so good.

To achieve consistency, I used this first triangle as a template and laid it against each of the rest of the pieces, drawing the cut line with my sharp pencil. It was then a simple case of lining up the cut line with the edge of the MDF jig, locking it down and cutting.

Cutting with the jig

Using the first triangle stave as a template

Lining up, ready to cut

The triangles cut

Setting the mitre angle

Gauging the line

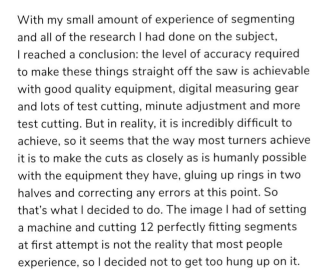
Planing the mitres on each stave

Using the scribble technique

With my small amount of experience of segmenting and all of the research I had done on the subject, I reached a conclusion: the level of accuracy required to make these things straight off the saw is achievable with good quality equipment, digital measuring gear and lots of test cutting, minute adjustment and more test cutting. But in reality, it is incredibly difficult to achieve, so it seems that the way most turners achieve it is to make the cuts as closely as is humanly possible with the equipment they have, gluing up rings in two halves and correcting any errors at this point. So that's what I decided to do. The image I had of setting a machine and cutting 12 perfectly fitting segments at first attempt is not the reality that most people experience, so I decided not to get too hung up on it.

MITRES

With the 12 triangles cut out, the next step was to add the mitre, which completes the compound angle. Straight away it was obvious to me that my usual bench vice is poorly situated for planing little triangles of wood like this, but fortunately I have a small engineer's vice fitted with wooden jaws.

I mounted this on a block which was held in my bench vice; this gripped each piece very securely and in a position that allowed me to plane them without getting in the way of my plane. Another advantage of this set-up was that it raised the height of the whole operation to a position that put far less strain on my back.

I used my digital protractor to measure the required 8.75° (once again, as close to 8.74° as I could measure), drawing this line on the end grain. Using this as a guide, I then set up my marking gauge to lightly score a line along the face of each segment, showing me where exactly I needed to plane to.

With the segments marked and my plane razor-sharp, I set about planing the mitres. I scribbled on each face to help me clearly see how the planing was progressing. As soon as I reached my gauge line and all of the pencil scribble was removed, I was done. A little wax on the sole of the plane helped to smooth the whole operation and after about an hour my segments were ready to glue.

Staves prepared and ready to glue

Gluing the staves

The two halves taped up and drying

GLUE-UP

The videos I watched during my research showed all sorts of elaborate ways of gluing up segmented work. Many showed the use of a glue gun to temporarily glue blocks on to each segment to give a clamping surface. I don't have a glue gun and I couldn't help feeling this method would make unnecessarily hard work of the job.

Based on my previous experience with segmenting (which was fairly limited) and my joinery background, I decided on a simpler approach. With my first attempt at segmenting, I had used a rub-joint to fix the segments together. This is where you add glue between two pieces and, while pressing them together with your fingers, rub them together, which forms a kind of vacuum between the two pieces of wood and holds them tight enough while the glue sets. This is an age-old, traditional technique and works well. On another staved project, I used masking tape as a flexible hinge to hold the pieces together while they dried. With the glue-up for this bowl, I decided to combine these two techniques.

I laid out six alternating segments, outside facing up, and joined them together with lots of masking tape, being careful to keep them closely held together throughout. I taped up both halves of the bowl, and double-checked that once they were put together the sapele and sycamore alternated all the way around the bowl. Now I was ready to add the glue.

I used a white wood glue, spread thinly and evenly between each join. More glue does not necessarily make a better joint, it's more about a good fit and an even coverage. Glue is not a gap filler.

I then folded the six segments together. The tape allowed me a little wiggle room so, while I pressed it all together with my fingers I gave each joint a little bit of movement, just enough to allow the glue to hold the joints. The glue I use has a quick 'grab' time, which was perfect as the glue grabbed and held itself while it set. I kept finger pressure on the glue-up for several minutes to allow the 'grab' to happen and, once satisfied, repeated the process on the second half.

JOINING

The two halves were left to dry overnight, then they were ready to join together. Obviously there was some work to be done on the join to get it to line up perfectly. As good as my planing is, there was always going to be a correction needed.

I decided the easiest option was to fix some 180-grit abrasive tightly to a board and rub the glue face against it until it was flat. Once again, I used a pencil scribble to track the progress of the sanding and once all of the pencil mark was removed, it was flat and ready to glue up.

With both halves flattened I evenly spread the glue, rubbed the two halves together to achieve the grab and added masking tape to hold it while the glue dried.

After leaving the glue to fully harden I carefully peeled off all the masking tape and looked over the joints. I was quite pleased that there were no real gaps and the whole thing felt completely solid. Strangely, the angle of the sides seemed much steeper than I had intended. I placed my protractor against the bowl and found the sides were nearer to 50° than the 35° I was aiming for. At this point I had no idea why this would be. It seemed unlikely that the chart was wrong, which meant I must have made a mistake. I double-checked everything I had done but couldn't work it out. It was only later that I realized my error, which was more a terminology problem than anything else.

To me, a mitre is the angle between each stave. The chart refers to a 'mitre angle' and a 'tilt angle'. I took the mitre to be, well, the mitre, and the tilt to be the angle of each side of the triangle. In fact, the chart refers to 'tilt' as the angle of the blade on a tablesaw, which is cutting what I call the mitre, so I had used the measurements the wrong way round. My tablesaw cuts should have been 8.74° and the planed mitre should have been 12.24°. Watching the video again proved this to be the case. However, there was no real harm done and I could get on with turning.

Sanding the glue faces flat

Using the scribble technique again

Not quite the angle I was expecting

Removing the wood below the spigot with a saw

Initial mounting of the blank, cutting the holding spigot

Turning the underside of the bowl

Turning the inside of the bowl using the wing of my spindle gouge and drawing the cut from the centre to the edge with the grain

Supporting the wall to minimize vibration while I turn

Finishing the base

TURNING THE BOWL

As the bowl was small, I chose a ½in (12mm) spindle gouge; tool overhang over the rest was minimal throughout the turning operation. The grain of the bowl, being staved, was most like spindle orientation so the cut was very even, without the changes between end and side grain as in normal bowl turning. I was quite comfortable doing this and achieved very good results. If you are more comfortable using a bowl gouge, then it would work equally well, and would indeed be a better choice if the bowl was bigger and the tool overhangs increase.

The only issue caused by my angle error was that the blank came to a point, with just a small dimple in the base, rather than there being a hole to fill later. Conveniently the dimple fitted the point on my live centre, so I mounted my faceplate, which permanently has a disc of MDF fixed to it, and sandwiched the blank between it and the live centre. I had to stroke my plane over the top of the bowl to ensure it sat flat against the MDF, but it worked well. Because the staves of the bowl were in spindle-turning orientation, I used my beading and parting tool to cut a chucking spigot and removed the remaining nub of wood using a handsaw with the lathe stationary.

I could then mount the bowl in the chuck, which held the staves together, giving me a little more confidence, and I made my first tentative cuts with a ½in (12mm) spindle gouge to the underside of the bowl. The cleanest cuts

were made by cutting with the wing of the gouge from the base, up to the rim. I gradually formed the sweeping curve I originally imagined.

Happy with the outside, I switched to the inside. Again, I used the wing of the tool and worked from the base up to the rim. I was pleased to see the centre of the bowl showed a neat join where all of the segments come together. I had initially thought I would need to make some sort of plug or base, but this was something of a happy accident.

As the bowl got thinner, there was a little vibration so I supported the wall with the fingers of my front hand. I checked the wall thickness and settled on ³⁄₁₆in (5mm). This seemed thin enough to give it a light appearance while being thick enough to leave strength in the joints between the staves.

Once satisfied, I sanded from 180 to 400 grit and removed the bowl from the chuck. I replaced the MDF disc on the lathe and remounted it as I originally had to tidy the base of the bowl.

To finish, I oiled the bowl with a hard wax oil and lightly buffed it to a sheen with a carnauba loaded buffing wheel.

CONCLUSION

This challenge really stretched my skills. I'm pleased with this little bowl and I learned a lot during the process.

Bowl from a board

The premise of this technique is to use a single board of thin timber to produce a much deeper bowl by cutting rings at an angle and then turn them into a bowl. Before making one, I had a rough idea of how it's done but I thought I'd have a chat with someone who knows more about it than myself first, so my first move was to contact an Instagram friend, Michael Mode (@woodmoder) who, among other things, specializes in making bowls using this technique. The effect has a lot of visual impact, especially when you consider how little wood is actually needed to make them. Unlike normal turning, where most of the blank is left on the floor as shavings, this technique creates very little waste. I planned to make one from a single timber and, if all went well, try a laminated board with several timbers.

SETTING OUT

There are two different ways to approach the bowl from a board technique: either to cut the rings on a bandsaw with the bed set at an angle, or to cut them out on the lathe. The issue with the bandsaw method is that each ring is made in two halves and need to be joined before cleaning and stacking, whereas the turning method seems more straightforward, so I decided to use this method.

I could visualize how I needed to cut the rings from the board to make them stack, but I needed to plan it out so I would know exactly where to cut and at what angle. I tried to draw it out on paper, full size, but when it came to working out the exact angles of the cut I struggled to get my head around it properly. After a couple of attempts I decided I needed more information and this time turned to YouTube.

After watching a video, I redrew my design. I picked a piece of 1in (25mm)-thick European oak, 9in (230mm) across, and drew out a rectangular cross section the same size. My standard chuck jaws need a 2¼in (56mm) tenon, so I started my drawing with a 2½in (60mm)-wide base. I only actually drew out one side of the bowl, so the drawing showed a radius of 4½in (115mm) – half of the 9in (230mm) diameter. With the radius of the base – 1⅛in (30mm) – taken from the overall radius, I was left with 3½in (85mm).

The next question I needed to answer was: 'How many rings/layers am I going to use?' One of the features of these board bowls, sometimes called 'economy bowls', is that they tend to end up conical in shape – which happens due to the process. However, I would like to try to get a little more shape into the bowl so it makes sense that making the rings a little more chunky would allow me to do this. I thought it should also give me a little more leeway to make mistakes on this first attempt.

If I divided my 3½in (85mm) into three (layers) it would give me rings with a wall thickness of around 1in (28mm), less the thickness of the tool I use, which is quite chunky, but would give me a bowl three times thicker than the original board and hopefully allow me to add some curve to the bowl.

To help me get my head around the angles I drew the three layers, marking the size of the base and ending up with a grid, on which I was able to connect the corners to show me the angle I to cut.

There's nothing like practical experience to clarify things, and with the small amount of wood that is at stake here, the cost of messing it up isn't actually that high, which I always find relieves some of the pressure.

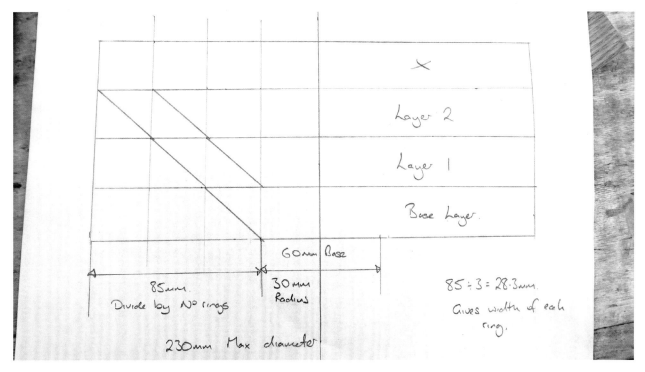

Drawing in full with working out

CUTTING THE RINGS

The first thing to address on any turning project is how to hold it. Most bowl projects begin on a screw chuck, but because there would be so little waste that wasn't an option here, so I sandwiched the oak disc between the chuck and live centre and turned a shallow tenon on the base using my ⅛in (4mm) parting tool. Some of the turners I'd seen online used a glue chuck to hold the bowl but I didn't see the need for that here.

With the tenon cut, I removed the disc and decided, for a little extra security, to add layers of masking tape to the back of the board and mount it on the chuck.

Theoretically this should make the parting-off less dramatic. With the oak disc on the chuck, I used my drawing to mark the positions of each ring and realized that by setting a sliding bevel to the angle shown on the drawing, I could use it to line up my parting tool at the beginning of the cut; I checked it periodically as the cut progressed. In this case the actual angle was 41°, although that will vary depending on the thickness and diameter of the blank and the number of rings being cut.

I used my ⅛in (4mm) diamond parting tool to minimize the waste and it sliced very cleanly. I do have a thinner tool, but it is a short-handled type and I much prefer the longer-handled tool.

In other projects, I have had to part work in a similar way and had no issues without the addition of the tape, but I thought the additional safety measure might be needed here. However, I found that, rather than making the cut safer and catching the ring as I completed the cut, it actually reduced the feel and changed the sound of the cut. I ended up misjudging it and cutting through faster than I expected. I found that the tape added no safety element to the operation.

Cutting at an angle towards the chuck makes the operation very safe in itself, because the ring physically can't come away from the rest of the blank and it falls on to the chuck, spinning and bouncing harmlessly until I stop the lathe. I could have removed the chuck and then the loose ring from the lathe, but instead I rested it safely on the bearing block, which is quite large on my old Wadkin. It sat there out of the way until I finished cutting the second ring.

Cutting the tenon

Marking the positions of the rings

Adding masking tape to the back of the disc

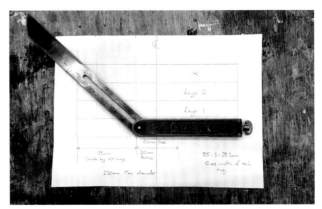

Setting the angle of the cut from the drawing

Using the sliding bevel to guide the angle of my cut

The first ring spins free safely behind the disc

Making the parting cut

Cutting the second ring with the first safely out of the way

GLUING THE BOWL BLANK

I now had a base block, which still had a chucking tenon on the underside, and two rings. The next job was to glue it up into a bowl blank. I found that by reassembling the sections back into its original board form, it was easy to line up the grain in the correct orientation. I then stacked them back into a bowl blank and made some marks to ensure I could line it all up during the glue-up.

The glue-up was the part that I felt could make or break this project. As Michael had pointed out during our discussions, if the rings slip with a single timber board, then it isn't the end of the world as it won't be very noticeable. However, if the rings slip with a board made of several timbers then it sticks out like a sore thumb and spoils the look of the bowl. The main advice Michael gave me was to not try to glue up too many layers at once, perhaps only one joint at a time, as it is increasingly difficult to get everything perfect with each additional layer. He suggested applying the glue and pressing them together with a weight on top until the glue begins to grab, and only then apply pressure with clamps. This made perfect sense to me as I've experienced similar issues when I've made segmented items.

CLAMPING

This is a job where having an extra hand would be a real benefit. As a little slip in a solid oak bowl would not be disastrous, I risked gluing the three layers in one hit. As advised, I applied the glue and rubbed the parts together lightly to encourage them to grab. I placed a heavy weight on top for a few minutes before adding boards to the top and bottom of the stack and gently adding four G-clamps to it. With the clamps loosely in position, I checked the layers of the bowl hadn't slipped, and gradually applied pressure to each clamp until there was even pressure holding it all together.

The rings in position with the grain lined up

Out of the clamps it is clear to see how it has slipped

Turning the outside

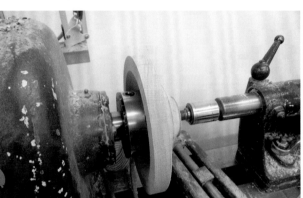
Bowl placed over the chuck with live centre holding it securely

Turning the inside

TURNING THE BOWL

I allowed the glue to cure overnight, then inspected the blank once it was out of the clamps. I had managed to align the two marks on the front of the blank but had neglected to look at the back and the top ring had slipped sideways somewhat. This wasn't a big problem on this bowl but I would need to take more care if I made a laminated version. Lesson learned though, so I should be more prepared next time.

I placed the bowl over the chuck and brought it up to the live centre, placing it in the centre mark from the original mounting. The base and central ring ran very true, but the top ring, which had slipped in the clamps, ran out by a good bit. I turned on the lathe and re-cut the tenon to make it perfect. I then brought the rim into line and began shaping the blank. There wasn't much scope to play with here, as the shape had to be some version of conical, but I tried to put in a sweeping curve from the base to the rim, which I was pleased with. I initially used a draw cut to remove the waste and form the shape, switching to the wing of my ³⁄₈in (10mm) (½in/13mm bar) bowl gouge in a shearing cut to refine the shape and leave a smooth surface ready

for sanding. I power sanded with 180 grit and then hand sanded to 400 grit before removing the tailstock and placing it in the chuck.

It was only as I hollowed the bowl out that I realized the combination of the ring slipping during the glue-up and my efforts to create a sweeping curve had left the wall of the bowl a little thin, and by the time I turned the inside with a sweeping curve to match the outside there was a little light shining through the side. My callipers proved that I was down to just ¹⁄₃₂in (1mm) at this point. I decided to finish the bowl anyway, obviously handling with great care. I thought I would prefer ¹⁄₈in (4mm) or ³⁄₁₆in (5mm) of wall thickness throughout. I reversed the bowl on my MDF disc mounted on a faceplate and brought the tailstock up again while I turned away the tenon down to a little nub, which I power sanded away at the end.

My first bowl from a board looked good (from a distance). I managed to achieve a fluid curve, rather than just a conical bowl, so I was pleased with that, and as Michael had predicted, the slippage on the plain bowl was not visible in the grain match but would be critical

Callipers prove it is a little thin

My first attempt

Removing the tenon

Laminating the different timbers

on a laminated board. The thin patch in the wall was unacceptable though and would have to be addressed on my next attempt. I put this one down as a learning bowl and got ready to make the final bowl from a board.

GLUE-UP
I decided this would be a good opportunity to use up some offcuts. I had some of the oak left from the first attempt, so I used that as the main timber with a stripe or two of contrasting wood. In the past, I've combined oak, walnut and sycamore before on a segmented bowl, so I knew they would work together. I found some suitable pieces and cut them down into strips. I liked the idea of an oak bowl with a stripe running through it. I cut a strip of walnut at 2in (50mm) wide, and a piece of sycamore 1⅛in (30mm) wide. I cut the oak blank at a random point that looked about right and placed the walnut and sycamore in. I felt something extra might be needed though, so I added a strip of ⅝in (15mm)-wide mahogany, which pulled it all together well. I planed the pieces smooth and then glued them together into a panel using three sash clamps and a good-quality white wood glue. While choosing the timber I was aware of the possible issue of colour contamination from different

timbers but all of these were close-grained timbers, apart from the oak, and the colours weren't too strong, so I was reasonably sure this wouldn't be a problem.

RINGS
The following day, with the glue fully cured, I flattened the panel using my planer and cut a disc of 12in (300mm) diameter. To work out the best size and angle for the rings I drew it out as I had before. The thickness was 1in (25mm) but I had more diameter to play with

Cutting the rings

Laminated bowl in clamps

Laminated bowl out of clamps and ready to turn

this time, meaning I had another decision to make. I had the ability to cut an extra ring this time, or I could stick to three rings, cutting them slightly wider, allowing me to add more shape into the bowl. The conical shape of this type of bowl has always been what I see as the downside to them. I would always rather have more shape than size so I opted for three layers, slightly wider than before, in the hope of achieving an improved sweeping curve without the daylight issue of the first.

As before, I used my drawing to mark out the rings and sliced them free with my ⅛in (4mm) parting tool and all went to plan. I didn't use masking tape this time but just took my time, carefully slicing the rings free from the disc. The rings stacked without a problem, the wide stripes of walnut and sycamore made lining them up quite easy, although it was obvious to me that they needed to line up perfectly otherwise the look of the bowl would be ruined.

This time I took Michael's advice and glued just two rings together at a time. I found the smallest two quite simple with very little slippage. Satisfied with their

position, I left them in clamps for a few hours before repeating the process for the larger ring later in the same day.

The larger diameter ring seemed to want to slip and slide more than the smaller rings but after much wrestling and a little swearing I was pleased with the look of it and, having learned from the first attempt, I remembered to check all around the glue-up rather than just the one face. Satisfied I had done all I could with this I left it overnight to fully dry.

TURNING

Out of the clamps, I was pleased with the look of the bowl blank. Everything seemed to be lining up well so the next stage was to turn it. I repeated the process from the first bowl, only this time being more aware of the wall thickness throughout. I placed the blank over the chuck and brought up the live centre to turn the underside and re-cut the tenon. I then sanded it all to 400 grit.

I reversed it in the chuck and checked the wall thickness with callipers; I found I had around ⁵⁄₁₆in (8mm) at the thinnest part, which gave me plenty to smooth over the join lines and mirror the flowing curve of the outside. I managed to achieve a pretty even ⅛in (4mm) wall thickness throughout. I was pleased that the stripes matched up well and the effect only improved as the bowl neared completion. Once I was happy with the finish from my bowl gouge on the inside I sanded through to 400 grit as I had before.

The final stage was to reverse-turn the bowl over my MDF disc with the live centre in place, lightly slicing away the tenon. After a final inspection of the bowl I applied three coats of hard wax oil.

Turning the inside of the bowl

CONCLUSION

I always enjoy projects that include different aspects of woodwork, so this one was a fun challenge for me. I'm glad that I went to the effort of making a practice bowl before making the laminated version as it allowed me to work out a few issues and resulted in a far better finished product. The thing I was most pleased about though was the amount of shape I managed to achieve in the bowl. I find the flowing curve very satisfying and was happy with my decision to opt for shape over size, as a taller bowl would certainly have been less shapely and more conical.

I think this style of bowl has a lot of scope and especially as thick-section seasoned timber is increasingly expensive and difficult to buy, the bowl from a board option becomes more and more attractive.

The finished bowl

BEYOND THE BASICS

Kylix

I was challenged to make something inspired by Ancient Greece. This was a pretty broad brief, so I decided to narrow it down a bit by focusing my research on Ancient Greek pottery. I liked many of the shapes I saw online, ranging from simple bowls to the familiar Greek vase shape, but the one I was particularly drawn to was a kylix, a low, open vase or perhaps a shallow bowl on a stem, a little like a tazza (a wide, shallow saucer). It included handles, which are always a challenge to turn, so I knew this was going to be a tricky piece to make.

RESEARCH

Through my online reading, I learned that a kylix was the most common drinking vessel from the time, used for drinking watered wine. It is quite odd-looking to modern eyes for a drinking vessel, but the second most commonly used vessel was called a kantharos, which is much more familiar as a handled goblet.

The inside of a kylix was usually painted with a scene, generally humorous, light-hearted or of a sexual nature. The image would be hidden by the wine and would only be revealed by drinking it.

The bowl of the kylix is a simple but beautiful curve but with a slight visual shift, while the curve from the underside of the bowl through the handles is a different but equally lovely line. I found this fascinating and couldn't wait to try to replicate it on the lathe. The problem was, despite the large number of examples I'd seen online, very few of them had their dimensions listed, and it is impossible to know the size of something without some form of reference point. With a little deeper digging, I was able to find specific examples of kylixes with their dimensions.

- The British Museum: 12¾in (325mm) diameter (16in/410mm including handles) and 4¾in (122mm) high
- The Metropolitan Museum of Art: 10⅛in (257mm) in diameter and 5in (124mm) high
- The Museum of Fine Arts in Boston: 8¼in (212mm) in diameter and just 3⅛in (78mm) high
- A private sale site: 8in (200mm) in diameter (11in/283mm with handles) and 5¼in (135mm) high

The sapele blank, ready for turning

I was surprised by how big they are and how difficult and impractical they seemed to be for drinking from, at least to my eye, compared to a modern cup or glass. At least I now had an idea of the sort of size it should be though, so I looked through my timber pile to see what might be suitable.

When I think of Ancient Greek pottery, I picture the red/brown colour of terracotta so in an attempt to mimic this I chose to use sapele, which is a similar red/brown colour. I had a board of 2⅝in (65mm)-thick sapele, 8¼in (210mm) wide. This was large enough for the bowl diameter but not the handles. The handles, however, are only on the end grain, so a rectangular block would give sufficient wood to do what I needed. The dimensions I found online suggest that the handles should be around 1⅝in (40mm) long each, so I cut the blank at a generous 11½in (290mm), drew a circle for the bowl at 8¼in (210mm), added an outer circle line to include the handles at 11½in (290mm) and cut it out on the bandsaw. At 2⅝in (65mm) thick it was only deep enough for the bowl, but a second disc of around 4–4¾in (100–120mm) diameter would work well for the foot and could be joined to the bowl later.

TURNING

The blank was a rectangle so was evenly balanced and I had no concerns about turning the odd shape. That said, the extended irregular shape meant I needed to keep my fingers on the tailstock side of the toolrest and could not check the wall thickness while the work was spinning. If you do feel uncomfortable with working like this, you could either try to find a larger blank from which you can cut a complete disc, or glue on sacrificial strips to form a full circle.

As with any bowl, I drilled a ⁵⁄₁₆in (8mm) hole for a screw chuck and mounted it on the lathe. I trued up the blank with my ½in (12mm) (⅝in/16mm bar) bowl gouge, moved to what would be the base of the bowl and began shaping. As I mentioned earlier, this bowl is a kind of two-shapes-in-one affair, so I began the curve as if I was turning a simple bowl shape and quickly adjusted the curve to form more of an ogee into the handles. Before long, I felt like I needed to reverse the blank to work from the top edge and continue the curve of both the handles and the bowl.

I turned a tenon on the base of the bowl for holding while hollowing, and allowed some extra wood which I could later use to achieve a perfect curve and give length to the tenon which will join the bowl to the base or foot of the kylix.

Turning the top of the handles was a little like turning a square bowl, so a steady hand and the heavy bowl gouge were needed to produce a smooth curve. As the rim of the bowl began to appear from the block of wood, I switched to my ½in (12mm) spindle gouge, which I find a better profile for working in the tight space between the rim and the handles.

Turning the underside of the bowl

Turning the top of the handles

Using the spindle gouge to shape the join between the rim and the handle

CHECKING THE CURVE

After stopping the lathe, adjusting and repeating a few times, I was satisfied that I was somewhere near where I wanted to be, but it was difficult to know for certain without breaking through the solid line of the handles, so I decided it was time to do just that. With a carving gouge I sliced through the solid wood and joined up the curve of the bowl in a small area of the side of the bowl and was very pleased to see that the curve looked just as I'd hoped.

At this stage I saw no need to do more carving, but I did still need to sand. With the possibility of having to reshape one side or the other there seemed little point in sanding until now. I flipped the bowl back into its initial screw chuck mounting and sanded the underside. As usual I used a combination of power and hand sanding, taking it from 180 to 320 grit and being extremely careful near the outside edge where the square edge could easily cause an injury.

Satisfied with the underside I remounted the bowl on the chuck and finished the top surface. I couldn't safely sand the top of the handles yet, but as much of this material was going to be removed there was little point anyway. I just took a light shearing cut with the wing of my spindle gouge to give a smooth tooled finish.

I then turned the inside of the shallow bowl. This was a straightforward bit of turning using my bowl gouge. I checked the wall thickness with my callipers from time to time to ensure a good, even thickness, allowing for a little extra timber at the bottom to allow for fixing to the base.

The shape of the bowl is difficult to see clearly ...

until I carve away some of the rim

Power sanding the underside of the bowl

Shear cutting the top of the handle for a clean surface

Hollowing the bowl

Marking out the handles

Cutting out the handles with my coping saw

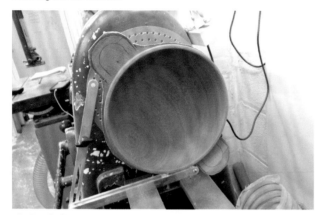
The bowl after removing the unwanted rim

The underside after removing the rim

Using a flat Microplane to blend the curve of the bowl

Power sanding to smooth the surface

CUTTING THE HANDLES

The handles posed the biggest challenge to me. I've read articles and seen demonstrators make various handled bowls such as a quaich (a Scottish/Celtic drinking bowl) but I've never tried it myself. I began by marking out the position of the handles. I estimated these were about 2½in (60mm) wide and used a pair of compasses to draw an even curve. I contemplated different methods of cutting, discounting the use of the bandsaw because held one way it would be difficult to see what I was doing, and held the other way it would be downright dangerous. I've also seen it done with a carving axe,

but I decided a coping saw would be the safest and most controllable option.

The bowl was difficult to hold steady while I sawed, so I added my indexer to the lathe to lock it tight while I sawed away the waste. This worked exactly as expected and left my turned bowl with handles at each end and just a thin strip of waste to remove between the base and rim of the bowl.

I chose a flat Microplane to remove this ring of waste and blend the curves, switching to a curved blade to blend the corner between the handle and the bowl. The finish from the Microplane was coarse compared to the rest of the sanded bowl, but it didn't tear the grain so it was ready for sanding. I used my cranked drill with a sanding arbor to work over the tooled area and blended the different textures into the smooth curve of the bowl using 180 grit. Happy with the surface, I swapped to a cork block with abrasive wrapped around it and hand sanded the same area with 180 to 320 grit until I was satisfied that there was no difference in the curve of the bowl where the waste wood had been.

ADJUSTING THE HANDLES

Having finished the rest of the bowl, the handles now looked a little long, and measuring them showed that they were longer than my intended 1⅝in (40mm), so I redrew the curves and set about shaping them properly. I removed most of the waste with the coping saw again, and used the flat Microplane to refine the shape further. I then used the angle drill again to sand them smooth, followed by hand sanding through the grits until I was happy with the shape, look and, perhaps most importantly, the feel of them.

Hand sanding to a final finish

The next step was to make the handles hollow. I chose to have the handles on the end grain of the bowl so the grain runs along the handle, giving as much natural strength as possible, but I didn't want to weaken them by removing too much wood from their centre. I began by drilling a ½in (12mm) hole and, using a small, round Microplane, I enlarged the hole until it could take a large, round Microplane. I then continued shaping until I was happy with the balance between a strong, usable handle and visually pleasing curves.

The handles now need re-marking ...

... and reshaping

Final hand sanding of the outside of the handles

Drilling the holes in the handles

Once again, the Microplane rasps left a coarse but sandable surface, so using strips of abrasive, I worked around the hole in the handles until they felt comfortable in the hand, working to 320 grit as before.

Using a Microplane to enlarge the hole

Sanding the hole

It's important to test the handle for comfort

THE BASE

I made the base from the same board of sapele so the grain would match up as closely as possible. I cut a disc of 4¾in (120mm) diameter and mounted it with my screw chuck, turning it to a cylinder and forming a holding tenon on the opposite face, just as I would for a bowl. I then turned a deep cove into it with my ½in (12mm) spindle gouge. This was slightly different from my normal way of working as the blank was a cross-grain bowl blank rather than a spindle blank, so I used the wing of the tool to shear cut, apparently uphill but in fact working with the grain. Once I was happy with the look of the base I returned to the bowl to turn a tenon to join the two parts together.

Turning the base

JOINING THE BASE TO THE BOWL

I used my usual method of remounting the bowl, holding it between a disc of MDF fixed to a faceplate and the live centre. I now knew how big to make the base of the bowl. I needed 3⅛in (80mm) of flat to sit on the base and I thought a 2in (50mm) diameter tenon would give a secure hold, so I needed to turn the remaining timber to form this.

Reworking the base of the bowl

Forming the mortise on the base

Test fitting

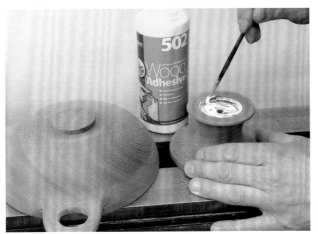
Gluing the two parts together

The finished kylix

Turning the bowl between centres like this gives me good access and a few cuts with my spindle gouge soon flattened the base. I used my skew as a scraper to make the tenon crisp and square. I then put the base back in the chuck. Having turned the tenon I just needed to cut the mortise to fit. I used my spindle gouge to remove most of the waste and my skew as a scraper again to crisply cut the side of the mortise and flatten its bottom. I test fitted the bowl and adjusted until I had a good, tight push fit.

The last job was to remove the holding tenon from the bottom of the base, which I did in the same way as before, between the disc of MDF and my live centre. Having the live centre in place meant I was left with a small pip, which I carved away and power sanded until it was smooth, then blended it with the rest of the base. I then spread glue in the mortise and, having carefully lined up the grain, pushed the two parts together. After leaving it to dry for a couple of hours, I applied the first of three coats of hard wax oil and my kylix was finished.

CONCLUSION

This project involved an interesting mix of techniques and I am quite pleased with the end result. I had never turned anything with handles like this before and I was surprised by how straightforward it was. I had imagined it to be far more challenging, although getting the curves of the bowl to meet properly did take some patience, forward planning and a little vision.

Looking critically at the finished kylix, the curve of the underside of the bowl could flow into the handles better, the base could be lighter and the handles could be more refined, but for a first effort I am satisfied and feel I have learned from the project, which is always a bonus. Looking again at images of kylikes online, they vary in shape so much that, even with the faults I've pointed out in my own work, mine would probably fit in well with the images and looks ready to be painted with a suitable Grecian scene.

Thread-chased bowl

Like most people, when I first began turning I had various phases where I tried out different techniques and subjects, trying to find my 'thing'. My box-making phase soon advanced into thread chasing, partly because John Berkeley was a member at my local turning club. John was known for his threaded puzzles and was a friend of Bill Jones, whose work I have always admired. Over the years I've had occasion to use the skill for some restoration purposes, but otherwise my chasers largely hang on my tool wall collecting dust. With this challenge, it was time to put them back to work.

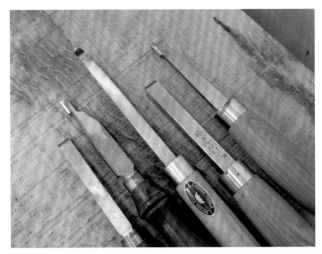
Thread-chasing tools

PLANNING

A faceplate project with screw threads immediately says to me: lidded bowl. I've never been that keen on lidded bowls if I'm honest. I rarely see a design that really works for me so I needed to find something that would work, but this was the least of my problems, the main one being that I really didn't think threads would cut on a faceplate blank. From my experience, threads only work on very dense woods, boxwood being a favourite, but looking for boxwood in sizes large enough for a lidded bowl is a little like looking for hen's teeth. While threads can be cut on other, less dense woods, it becomes hard work and they will often crumble because of the grain structure, giving them no strength or longevity.

On a cross-grain bowl, where there is a repeat of side and end grain and there are always those two coarse patches either side of the end grain, I was struggling to imagine that a thread would hold. The only way I could see it might work was by using a much coarser thread than is usually used for box making.

Luckily, I have a pair of chasers of 8tpi, along with my standard set of Crown chasers at 18tpi. New and vintage Thread chasers are available in a wide range of sizes online. Search for 'hand thread chasers' in your favourite search engine or auction site and there is usually a good selection that will come up. My old lathe had a 1in x 8tpi spindle nose and I liked the idea of making my own fittings for it. In reality, however, a chuck is so versatile at holding things I never actually used them for that purpose – in fact, I had to fit them with handles especially for this project.

PRACTICE

My first job was to practise thread chasing and see if I could remember how to do it. I mounted a piece of boxwood in the chuck and had a go with my 18tpi set. I remember John Berkeley saying that the finer teeth are easier to use, so I started with the outside tool, which I always used to find easier to use. After a couple of attempts I found the rhythm and soon had fine shavings coming from the tool. I hollowed out the centre of the blank and tried the inside chaser with the armrest tool. Once again, after a couple of failed starts I managed to find the rhythm and make a clean thread. I parted off the hollowed section, sized the remaining piece of boxwood and cut another outside thread to match. Cutting threads is one thing, making a matching set is a whole other problem. After a few attempts and much adjustment, I managed to make the two fit together. A promising start. I then switched to the 8tpi set. With these, it was far more difficult to get a start to the thread, but once they picked up the thread, they cut almost as easily as the finer set. Oddly, I found the inside thread a little easier than the outside with the 8tpi, I'm not sure why, but again I managed a thread.

Chasing the inside thread

Chasing the outside thread

The matching threads

8tpi practice on boxwood

TECHNIQUE

The actual technique for thread chasing is easier to show than to explain, but I'll have a go. If you can get hold of copies of Bill Jones' *Notes from the Turning Shop* and John Berkeley's *All Screwed Up!*, they're worth a read and explain the techniques involved. The main thing to understand is that the chasers have the thread ground into them, so once the first cut is made, they pull themselves across the surface of the wood. Unlike most turning tools where the turner has to move and manipulate the tool, you have to resist this urge with thread chasers and let the chaser do the work and only really apply some pressure into the wood. The resulting motion is kind of circular, as the tool engages in the thread and is pulled to the left, you then withdraw the tool, move it back to the right-hand end and repeat. All of this is done at slow speed – I use the lowest on my Wadkin at 220rpm.

CHASERS

Chasers are scraping tools, so can be a little harsh, but as long as they are presented pointing downward slightly and are kept sharp, which is done by simply touching the top edge on the grinder, they cut well. The addition of a little paste wax to the area being chased can also help the tool run smoothly across the surface.

Using the male/outside chaser first as it's usually the easiest to get to grips with, cut a tenon and add a chamfer to the leading edge. Using the teeth in the centre of the chaser presented to the chamfer, move the tool in the circular motion I described earlier. Often the first few attempts will just scratch at the wood, but persevere and after a couple of passes the beginnings of a thread will start. As soon as the tool pulls itself through the wood continue to repeat the circular motion but without forcing that sideways movement, and gradually bring the handle round so that it's square to the wood and the thread is cutting along the tenon you have cut.

The female/inside chaser works in the same way but there are two ways of using it. I have always used an armrest tool by Crown, which sits on the toolrest and supports the chaser. This is the way Bill Jones used to do it, and when looking at how things should be done, I will always look at the methods the best people use – there aren't many better than Bill. Alternatively, you can bring the toolrest across the work and rest the chaser directly on it. This feels more conventional to the modern turner but I find it a little restrictive as I'm now used to the armrest tool. The armrest tool is nothing more than a long handle with a steel shaft with a little L-shaped upstand on the end. The handle tucks under the left arm, the metal shaft sits on the toolrest and the fingers of the left hand pinch the chaser to the armrest tool. Cutting the thread is much the same as for the outside.

A chamfer needs to be cut; the centre of the teeth is used to begin the thread on that chamfer. Once the tool is pulling itself across the wood, the handle of the chaser can be brought round to parallel with the thread and it can be fully cut. As with the outside, the only real pressure is applied by pulling the armrest and chaser toward the thread as that circular motion is repeated.

TESTS ON CROSS-GRAIN

Before I began work, my expectation was that, mostly, the threads cut into cross-grain wood would be OK on the side grain and crumbly at best on the end grain. I thought I would have to support the fibres of the wood with sanding sealer or, more likely, thin CA glue to even get close to an acceptable thread, even on a close-grained timber. In short, I was not hopeful of a positive outcome.

The blanks cut for my tests

I selected four pieces of wood from species I had around the workshop in suitable sizes: American black walnut, sycamore, sapele and European oak. Walnut and sycamore have the finest grain and possibly stood the best chance of any sort of success. I felt oak was far too coarse and I expected the worst results from that, but I wanted to prove this to myself so I included it in the test. Sapele is a reasonably close-grained wood but the grain does interlock somewhat, which could lead to problems. I cut a 4in (100mm) disc of each and mounted them on a screw chuck, one by one, to see what would happen. On each disc I cut the outside thread first, followed by an inside thread. The results couldn't have surprised me more.

SYCAMORE

I began my tests with the sycamore sample, which I felt stood the most chance of success. I cut the thread all the way across the 1½in (40mm) thickness of the blank and stopped the lathe. The side grain was crisp and sharp and as I rotated the lathe to search for the crumbled end grain I was amazed to find that, although it was a little more coarse than the side grain, the end grain was still almost as crisp as the side. Excited by this discovery, I hollowed the inside around 1in (25mm) deep and struck a thread on the inside. Just as on the outside, while the end-grain areas were a little coarser than the sides, they were remarkably clean and far, far better than I ever expected they could be.

Chasing the outside thread on the sycamore blank

The results were good on the side grain

Almost as crisp, even on end grain

Chasing the inside thread in sycamore

The result of the inside thread

Walnut outside

Walnut inside

Oak outside

Oak inside

Sapele inside

WALNUT, OAK AND SAPELE

I repeated the test on the walnut with similar results. If anything, I found it cut a little easier than the sycamore, although this could have been down to more practice and having 'the knack' by now.

Next, I tried the oak. Although I was a little more hopeful than I had been, I still expected a pretty crumbly thread but to my amazement, even on this piece of oak, the threads were clean. If I could cut threads on an actual project this cleanly I would be more than happy.

Lastly, I tried the sapele. This was the most difficult of the four to cut. The chaser just didn't want to slide along it like it had the others and, even with it freshly sharpened and a little wax added, it was more of a battle to achieve a thread. That said, I did manage to cut a thread, but this was the least crisp of them all.

THE DESIGN

These tests confirmed that I could cut a thread on a cross-grain blank and suddenly a whole world of possibilities opened up. One of the things that had put me off thread chasing all those years ago had been the very few woods that would easily accept a thread, but if I could cut a cross-grain thread on almost any wood, that was very exciting indeed.

Of course, now I had to put this into a project. I needed to find a lidded bowl design that I could work with. I am a keen user of Instagram and whenever I see something I particularly like I save it for later reference, which is a very useful tool on the app. I checked my saved pictures and found one of a lidded bowl by Iranian turner Azadeh Masoumi (@azadeh_msm). Azadeh kindly agreed to let me replicate the design. Her original has a simple lift-off lid, but I thought it would work well with a screw lid.

I checked my timber stocks and selected a piece of 3in (75mm) walnut and cut a 6in (150mm) disc for the bowl. I decided a contrasting sycamore lid would work well, so cut a similar disc from some 1½in (40mm) stock. These would be tied together with a walnut finial.

Working the outside of the bowl

Turning the inside of the bowl

TURNING THE BOWL

The walnut turned beautifully, a light shearing cut producing lovely, fine, chocolate shavings and, after sanding to 400 grit, the wood glowed even before an oil was applied. This shape was new for me, but it was relatively simple and, on the outside at least, a joy to turn.

With the outside done, I flipped the bowl over and held it on the chucking tenon to hollow it. I ran the options through my mind before fully committing, but decided the best course of action would be to turn the bowl fully and sand it, leaving an area slightly thick in which to cut the thread. I could cut the thread quite early on in the hollowing phase, but as with any work like this, it would be too easy to damage the thread, either with a misplaced tool, careless sanding or, worse, a catch.

I cut a curve into the rim of the bowl and a small ledge for the lid to sit on, leaving an area below this for the thread. I then moved on to hollow the bowl. This was slightly tricky with the bulbous shape but by monitoring the wall thickness with callipers and using my steep angled bottoming gouge I was able to create a smooth flowing curve from beneath the thread to the bottom. I then sanded through to 400 grit as I had on the outside.

CHASING THE THREAD

Now for the moment of truth: could I cut a thread when it actually matters? As is often the case, the additional pressure we put on ourselves as turners when working on an important project can be the biggest barrier to success, so after a couple of rough starts I managed to relax and cut a good thread. I found adding a little paste wax very helpful here. I experienced a little vibration in the wood which I hadn't expected, although it shouldn't have been a surprise considering I was working near the rim of a hollowed bowl. Being critical (as I always am with my own work), it wasn't the best thread, but I thought it would be crisp enough to work.

Satisfied with the bowl, I mounted the piece of sycamore on a short screw chuck and cut a chucking tenon on the top, flipping it over into the chuck to cut the thread. I measured the lid tenon, which would take the thread, against the thread in the bowl and cut it slightly over size, both in length and diameter, and made a start on the thread. This one went much more smoothly and once the thread was cut I tried the bowl against it. The thread began the grip and then quickly tightened. On closer inspection I realized the tenon wasn't completely straight, so I adjusted it and re-cut the thread. I brought up the bowl and adjusted the fit and the diameter of the lid a few more times before the fit was just right.

I shortened the threads on the lid a little as no one wants to spend too long unscrewing a lid, no matter how well the threads have been cut. By pure luck, the grain of the lid and bowl lined up perfectly, although this was relatively easy to adjust by cutting the shoulder above the thread on the lid.

Waxing the thread to smooth the cut

Chasing the thread

The finished thread

Cutting the thread on the lid

Testing the fit of the threads

TURNING THE LID

Happy with the threads, I hollowed the underside of the lid to reduce the weight a little and to maximize the storage space inside the bowl, although I didn't go too far as I knew the finial would need to fit into the lid as it will be used to unscrew the lid.

I turned the lid over and mounted it as I always do to remove a tenon from the underside of a bowl, bringing the tailstock up and sandwiching it between the centre and a disc of MDF on a faceplate. I was able to turn a smooth dome into the lid and remove the tenon, sanding it to the same 400 grit as the rest of the bowl. I took the lid to the drill press and drilled a $5/16$in (8mm) diameter hole into the mark left.

Turning the top of the lid

Turning the finial

The finial was a simple bit of spindle turning, taking care to cut a tight-fitting tenon where it joins the lid. I cut an angle on to the end of the finial carefully on the bandsaw and sanded it smooth to 400 grit. I added some glue into the hole and fit the finial, which was slightly chunkier than Azadeh's as it will be used to unscrew the lid.

I applied three coats of Treatex hardwax oil to it, using a brush to ensure the threads were well oiled, followed by a light buff on my dome brush.

Fitting the finial

Oiling the bowl, brushing into the threads

The threads finished with oil

CONCLUSION

I can't express my surprise enough over how well the threads cut into the cross-grain blanks. In my mind there was no way this would work but I was really pleased with how this turned out. The shape of the bowl is very pleasing and the contrast between the walnut and sycamore is lovely. It will be interesting to see how this ages and if it moves, as this is always a potential issue with threaded work. For the same reason, I didn't want to go too big with a threaded project. In an ideal world I suppose this would be rough turned and left for a few weeks to truly settle, but this isn't always viable. Perhaps I need to experiment with thread chasing on this type of work more and I might yet find 'my thing'.

The finished lidded bowl

Square platter

I was challenged to make a square bowl or platter and, in theory, the process of turning a square bowl should be largely the same as turning a standard round bowl, but the corners may cause difficulties. A sharp gouge, presented correctly, combined with the correct lathe speed and a smooth movement should solve nearly all of these problems. That's the theory of making a square platter, but how did this stack up against the practice of actually doing it? I had made one, very early on in my turning career, but it was an ugly thing. This time I planned to make a much better job of it.

DESIGN

Usually, with my production work, I have a CAD drawing or a master part to work from. But here I could make whatever design I liked – as long as it was square! It's always tempting to jump in with both feet and make something highly decorative and detailed, but I strongly believe that, for your first attempt at any form of turning, keeping the design simple makes life much easier. Once you understand the techniques, you can then start adding extra detail.

Flicking through some of my books, I found a square 'sushi-style platter' in Mark Baker's book *Woodturning Projects* that appealed to me. It was square and simple, with an elegant curve and good overall balance to it. I decided to use the proportions of this design as a basis for my bowl, just adding a beaded foot because I'm a sucker for a foot on a bowl.

DEALING WITH THE CORNERS

Throughout this project, I knew that the corners of the bowl would cause problems. I remembered from my earlier attempt that, unlike a round bowl with a diameter of 9¾in (250mm), if you cut a 9¾in (250mm) square bowl, its diameter will actually be the measurement across the corners, which is roughly one and a half times more than the straight face. So, if your lathe capacity is 9¾in (250mm), don't cut a 9¾in (250mm) square – it won't fit! You need to cut about a 6½in (165mm) bowl to fit a 9¾in (250mm) lathe.

Fortunately, my lathe has capacity for a 15½in (400mm) bowl, so my ash blank would not be a problem. Like Mark Baker's original, I've gone for a blank of 9¾in (250mm) square, 14in (350mm) across the corners.

I cut the blank on my tablesaw with a fine cutting blade. This gave a perfectly square cut and left a surface that needed very little cleaning up. I realized that centring the bowl was an important part of the initial mounting, unlike a round bowl where any slight misalignment can be turned away in the early stages. If a square bowl is slightly off-centre it can affect the appearance of the finished item, showing up as a variable thickness on the square edge. I carefully marked the centre of the blank and fit a faceplate ring. I found it difficult to visualize the end result at this point, so I decided that the shorter multiple screws of a faceplate ring were preferable to a single larger fixing of a screw chuck. There's nothing worse than your initial fixing showing on the finished bowl.

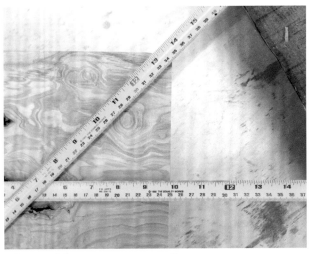
Take note of the measurement across the corners on a square bowl to ensure it fits on your lathe

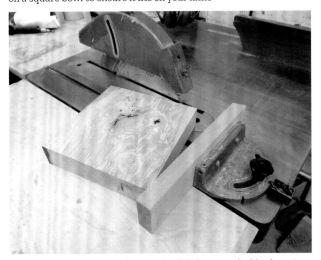
Using a saw bench with a fine-toothed blade to cut the blank to size

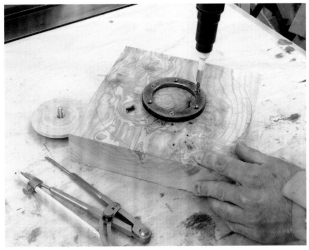
Carefully fitting the faceplate ring to the blank

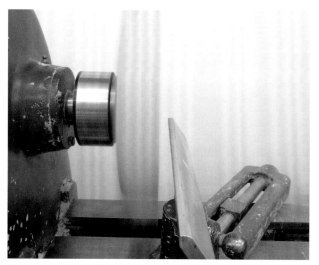

Check the corners of the blank won't hit your toolrest or banjo before turning on the lathe

EXTRA CHECKS

It is good practice to check your work turns freely before pressing 'start', but with square bowls it is vitally important. Positioning the toolrest and banjo in just the right place is essential to avoid damaging the blank before you have even picked up the bowl gouge. Check, and check again.

When you do press 'start', the spinning corners can be quite alarming, both in the sound they make and the amount of air they move. Start at a low speed and work up; once again this is best practice in general, but is all the more important here. I worked at 960rpm throughout this project, slowing to 750rpm for the final reverse turning operation.

PRACTICE CUTS

I left my blank deliberately a little over-thick so I could practise the cuts needed throughout the process. It is easier to practise when you have spare wood than when you are down to your last few millimetres on the inside

... and the push cut ...

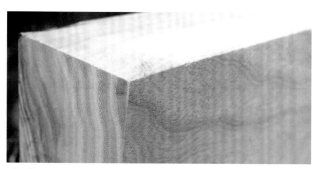

... both gave encouraging results

Finding the ideal position for the bowl gouge with bevel rubbing

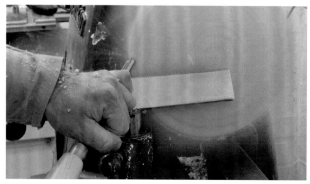

An early practice with the pull cut ...

Using a push cut to form the curve on the underside of the bowl

of a bowl. The cuts I used were the push cut, the pull (draw) cut and the shear cut. At various points on any bowl project, I will use all of these cuts. On this project, I wasn't entirely sure how the corners would affect these cuts.

Breakout was my biggest concern on this bowl. It would have been possible to fix sacrificial blocks to the sides, essentially making it a standard round bowl, but I wanted the challenge of turning it square. I would just have to deal with any breakout, one way or another. I tried each of the cuts to see which would be better at protecting the edges, and the early signs were good with each.

My preference for roughing the underside of any bowl is the pull cut. As I knew I would need a push cut on the inside of the bowl, I decided to give this a try on the underside too. Bevel position is much more critical for the push cut, so I used the solid portion of the bowl to find where my bevel rubs and then used that tool position to cut in from the edge.

The wings initially bounced the bowl gouge around a lot, too much to make a smooth cut. After trying a few variations of the cut, I got much better results by taking a slightly bigger and more positive cut than from trying to be too gentle and overly cautious. The fact that the edge is properly engaged in the wood gave me control, much like cutting a bead with a skew. If you are too cautious, the chances of a catch increase significantly.

The next cut I tried was a push cut to add shape to the underside of the bowl. A few different variations of presentation were needed to get it right, but it worked. I am much more comfortable with the pull cut, so I switched back to that for the majority of the shaping. I feel it is easier to allow the wood to come to the tool with the pull cut. With the push cut, the temptation is to apply too much pressure, which causes problems with bevel bounce.

CHECKING PROGRESS

As the shaping progressed, I kept stopping the lathe to check the shape and the square edges, to ensure I wasn't chipping out. Usually, you can check the curve of a bowl while it spins, both visually and by touch, but the corners of the square bowl make this impossible, so the only answer is to stop the lathe.

Two problems emerged as I worked, but as I was frequently stopping and checking my progress, I was able to head them off before they became real issues.

CHIPPING OUT

The first issue to sort out was a section of the square edge that was chipping out rather than cutting cleanly. This problem was exacerbated by the grain pattern. My solution was to employ a joinery technique: a sharp block plane was used to put a slight chamfer on the edge in question, reducing the harshness of the gouge cut on the edge.

The chipped edge

My solution was to plane a small chamfer on the edge

PERFECTING THE CURVE

The second problem I found with the square bowl was the lack of tool support over the wings. As there was less wood beneath the tool, if I applied a continuous amount of pressure to the wood throughout the cut, the gouge removed more wood from the wings and the curve became uneven. After a few experimental cuts I realized I would have to change my approach slightly. I continued with the pull cut, but applied slightly more pressure, tool to toolrest.

Flexing a steel ruler around a curve will help show up an imperfect curve

I positioned myself so I could make the full cutting movement in one go, without having to adjust my footing. I tried to visualize the shape continuing in a smooth curve as I worked. By focusing on my movement, keeping it smooth and fluid and the extra stability of the increased tool-to-toolrest pressure, I was able to make the cut smoothly, without the change of shape I had been experiencing previously.

A great way to check the quality of a curve is to use a length of flexible material. In this case I used a steel ruler, and flexed it across the surface of the bowl. Material such as the thin steel of a ruler will always flex into a perfect fluid curve, so by flexing it against the curve of the bowl you can see how good it looks.

FINISHING CUTS

With the curve looking good and the edges finished crisply, I needed to take a couple of finishing cuts to leave a perfect surface ready for sanding. I had two main options for this: a push cut or a shear cut. My preference is nearly always a shear cut. The body position needed for a shear cut allows great visibility of the overall shape of the bowl, unlike the push cut, which I sometimes find restrictive. Also, the tool is against my body throughout the shear cut, so I have better tool control.

Shear cutting the surface

Having perfected my body movement to cut the curve with the pull cut, the slight change of presentation to the shear cut made it easy to continue the same sweep and finish the underside of the bowl. A shear cut uses no bevel contact, just a razor-sharp edge, presented at around 45° to the surface. It looks and feels a little strange to begin with because the flute is almost facing the wood, but the fine shavings that are produced show how well this cut works.

Hand sanding the accessible areas

Using the orbital palm sander to smooth the wings

SANDING

Great care is needed when sanding square bowls; those wings are very unforgiving to anything put near them. My preference for sanding bowls is always to combine hand and power sanding, which I find gives the best control and surface finish. In this case, I sanded the solid centre section with standard hand-sanding techniques. Then, with the lathe stopped, I used an orbital palm sander to smooth and blend the wings. I finished with abrasive on a cork block, sanding with the grain to 320 grit. I also took this opportunity to sand the edges of the bowl.

TURNING THE INSIDE

With the bowl turned around in the chuck, I drew a pencil line of the curve I was aiming for. Mark's original bowl was only ¼in (5mm) thick; I decided that there was little point making my first square bowl any more difficult than it needed to be and I'm not keen on overly thin bowls. So I aimed for a consistent measurement of around $5/16$–$3/8$in (8–10mm). I marked this on two faces and I was pleased that I could see these marks quite clearly while turning.

The curve of the bowl marked on the edge

Initial cuts going well

Shaping cut in action

The curve of the bowl develops

The curve of the wings is easily monitored visually

Once inside the solid section, callipers are needed to check the thickness is even

I deliberately left extra waste wood above the final surface for a few more practice cuts. As before, positive cuts worked best, moving forward steadily and smoothly. The technique I used here is particularly suited to thin-walled, large or wet wood bowls. Starting at the rim, the cuts focus on the shape, thickness and finish of the first inch of the bowl. Once this is done satisfactorily, the cut can progress to the next inch and so on until the turning is complete. The main advantage of this technique is that the bulk of the bowl remains for as long as possible, helping to resist flex and movement before it is absolutely necessary. I also find that, because my focus is on a particular area, it gives me the best chance of achieving a consistent wall thickness without cutting through the bowl.

Regular checks were needed and once the cut was within the solid portion of the bowl, I used callipers to maintain an even wall thickness. The turning at this stage became just the same as for any other standard bowl.

SANDING AGAIN

As always, there was more sanding required and the process was similar to sanding the outside. I power sanded the solid portion, then switched to my cranked drill to power sand the wings with the lathe stationary. This cranked drill is easier to use single-handed than a normal drill. The sanding was finished off with abrasive wrapped around a cork block, as before. The square edges were incredibly sharp, so I softened them with 320 grit.

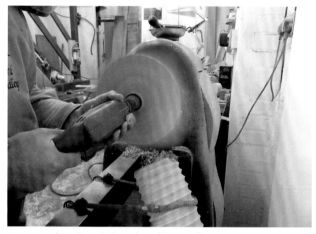
Power sanding the solid portion of the bowl

Using the cranked drill to blend the wings

REVERSING THE BOWL

The reversing was done using the same technique I use for all my bowls except I couldn't use the MDF disc as only the tips of the corners would be in contact, so instead I padded the chuck with folded paper towel and held the bowl between this and the live centre, essentially between centres, turning away the holding spigot. The tiny nib that was left was then carved and sanded away. I finished the bowl with several coats of hard wax oil.

CONCLUSION

I enjoyed making this bowl, which threw up some interesting challenges, all of which I was able to solve using techniques that I already knew from various areas of turning and woodworking. I think this proves, if proof were needed, that having a good and wide knowledge of techniques is the best base for making any turned project.

If I were to make this again, I would have a better understanding of how the shape is formed and the relationship between the initial blank and the end result. On this bowl I lost a lot of the olive ash colour and figuring because of this lack of vision and understanding. Next time I would hope to maximize this timber better, but overall I am pleased with the outcome.

The bowl reversed over the chuck

Turning away the chucking tenon

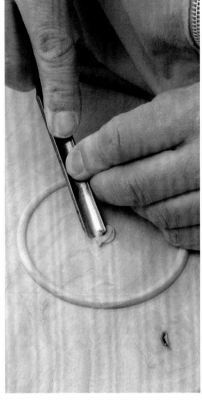

Removing the nib with a carving gouge

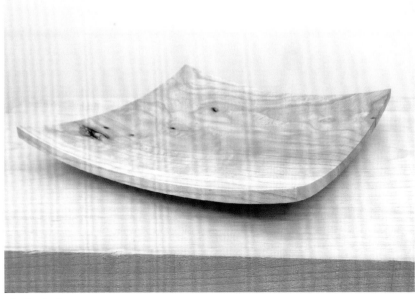

The finished item

Jigsaw bowl

Many of us spent time with jigsaw puzzles during the Covid lockdown, and that was the inspiration behind this challenge. I decided to make a small, shallow bowl or platter made of four sections, each interconnected with the familiar jigsaw links. Making it a square bowl would give it a more easily recognizable jigsaw look, too.

MAKING A START

After making a few sketches I had a good idea of what I would make. I had a few concerns over the strength of the cross-grain sections, but once glued together as a solid piece, they should be fine. Achieving tight-fitting joints would be the biggest challenge.

I planned to use 3in (75mm) squares of walnut and sycamore – a winning combination if ever there was one – to produce a roughly 6in (150mm) square bowl. After sorting through my timber pile I found suitable sections of timber and planed them to 1⅜in (35mm) thick, which should be enough to produce a pleasing curve in a square bowl.

After playing around with some offcuts of walnut, I decided the easiest way to achieve the familiar jigsaw link would be to drill a hole and cut into it to form the hollow, then, using techniques similar to cutting dovetails, I could 'draw' around the hole with a knife and cut out the 'tail' (using dovetailing terminology) part of the jigsaw, paring it to fit. I made up a sample, which wasn't perfect but showed great promise for my idea.

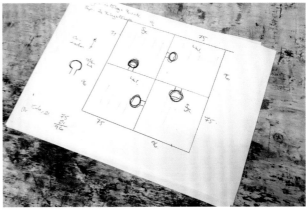

Initial sketch of the jigsaw bowl

The squares each needed to be 3 x 3¾in (75 x 96mm), which allows for the protruding part of the jigsaw. I numbered the parts and marked out the centres and positions of the pins and tails using a mortise gauge. I used a ⅝in (15mm) lip and spur drill in the pillar drill, which cut lovely clean holes. I then cut a ⁵⁄₁₆in (8mm)-wide space into the hole to form the jigsaw shape. Sitting squares of wood on top of each other and using a knife, I marked the tail on the next piece and took it to the bandsaw to rough it out.

Walnut sample to test the principle

Marking the shape with a knife

Marked out and ready to cut

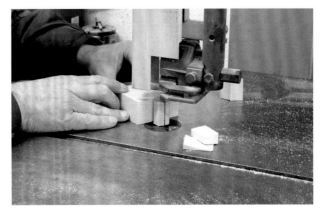

Cutting out on the bandsaw

Jigsaw part rough-cut on the bandsaw

Paring with a carving gouge

The parts look promising partly fitted together

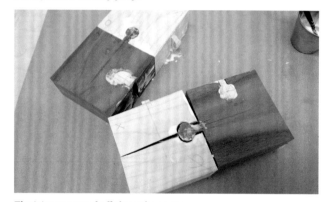
The joints snapped off along the grain

PARING

With the shapes roughed out, I used an old technique, which some may see as a cheat for dovetail making. I clamped a square piece of wood in place, directly over the scored line of the shoulder, and pared down, using the wood as a guide to achieve a dead square and clean cut. I did this on the shoulders and on the stem of the jigsaw tail. For the rounded part of the tail, I used a carving gouge with a similar shape to the diameter of the drill and pared down until I was happy with the look of it all. I offered the two halves of the jigsaw together and, although I didn't fit it fully – there was great potential for it jamming and me not being able to get it apart – but partially, I was happy with this.

I repeated the process on all four of the jigsaw details and spent a very enjoyable morning cutting and paring the joints until it was time for assembly.

JOINT FAILURE

Satisfied that everything seemed to be lining up well and the jigsaw parts were all beginning to fit together, I was ready to add some glue and assemble my bowl blank. I placed a piece of brown paper on my bench to avoid spreading glue everywhere and set up with my glue and brush.

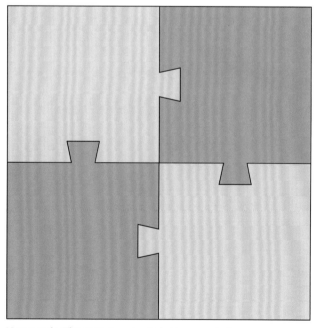
Not to scale. The grain runs top to bottom on all pieces.
The walnut sections are 3⅜in (87mm) long and 3in (75mm) wide, the sycamore sections are 3in (75mm) long and 3⅜in (87mm) wide to allow for dovetails

I spread glue on the first joint and tapped it together with my mallet. I was very pleased with how it was going – if they all went this well, it would be an easy assembly. However, as I tapped the second together the cross-grain tail snapped clean off. You can imagine some of the choice words that came from my mouth at this point. After a look at it, I decided that as long as the other joints went together well, I should be able to glue it back together as it was a break along the grain. Unfortunately, as I tapped the next joint together, the entire section of sycamore split along the grain. In some sort of desperate attempt to get something from my morning's labours, I tried the last joint, which snapped off along the grain, just as the second had. What a disaster!

At this point, I had some decisions to make. Should I spend another half day repeating the process, making the joints much looser and hope it works the second time? With several deadlines looming, I didn't have time to deal with another failure. I needed a Plan B.

I ran through alternatives that used the same principle but would stand a better chance of success. I had been using dovetailing techniques so far; maybe if I used a dovetail

New blanks with a fresh drawing, ready for Plan B

router cutter, which would produce regular and pretty reliable shapes, I could make the same bowl, but use dovetails as the joining feature rather than the jigsaw links. I liked the idea, but didn't have a dovetail cutter. Luckily, I was able to borrow a suitable one from a local joiner.

DOVETAILS
I cut more squares of sycamore and walnut, opting for a slightly thinner 1⅛in (28mm) this time. The dovetails only protrude by ½in (12mm), limited by the cutter design, so my new blanks were 3 x 3⅜in (75 x 87mm).

Routing the dovetails produces a good shape and a lot of smoke

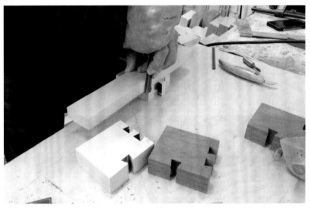
Paring the waste away

Ready for the glue-up

One of the sycamore tails has a chip, but it shouldn't be a problem

I had never actually cut dovetails on a router, but I understood the principle. The main thing to know about routing dovetails is that you shouldn't just cut straight through with the cutter, as it is a heavy cut to make in one pass. Unlike straight or even chamfer cutters, you can't take several passes as the dovetail shape doesn't allow it, so it has to be done in one hit. To make it easier on the router and the cutter, a channel is cut with a straight cutter first, so it has less material to remove and there is less stress on both the cutter and the wood. I did this in the centre of the space in between the pins and each side of the tails, before swapping to the dovetail cutter.

My router table set-up is fairly rudimentary; the fence is planed softwood, clamped to the table, and I use a square of plywood as a pusher – it has lots of contact with both the fence and the work so is very stable and offers full support to the work throughout the cut. I feel comfortable doing this, but you might have a different set-up you could use.

The tool I had borrowed was not a premium cutter, as it was part of a mixed set of commonly used router bits. As I worked it produced quite a bit of smoke, even after I honed the carbide tips with a diamond file, but the surfaces it produced were clean and smooth, if a little charred.

I cut the pinholes first so I could adjust the fit of the tails and get them perfect. I used my marking knife to mark the exact positions of the tails and made my initial cut slightly wide of the mark, allowing me to adjust my fence and creep up to the perfect fit. Once I was satisfied with the first, I cut the rest of the tails.

I removed the waste wood on either side of the tails on the bandsaw and pared it flat and square using the guide block technique I had used earlier. As I was routing the tails, one of the sycamore blocks chipped out – there must have been a curl in the grain causing a weakness or short grain – but I didn't think this would cause a problem as I could align it to the inside of the bowl and it should turn away.

Gluing up the joints

GLUE-UP

Glue-ups are always a little stressful, and this one was even more so after my earlier failure. This time though, the joints slipped together much more easily and I needed no more than a light tap with my mallet to close up the last one. The tightrope I was walking here was between joints that are very tight and need persuading to go together with a mallet – but also risk splitting the wood, as I'd found earlier – and being too loose and gappy. These dovetails fell slightly on the looser side of this imaginary line, so I decided, having liberally glued every surface, to add some clamps while the glue cured. The clamps squeezed out a little glue, proving it was the right decision.

In clamps to dry

TURNING THE BLANK

Having been left to dry overnight, the dovetailed blank was now ready to turn. I used a faceplate ring for my initial mounting, ensuring there was a screw into each of the four quadrants that made up the blank. I was confident that the blank would hold together perfectly well, but a little extra insurance never hurt anyone. The screws are ¾in, No.8 (4 x 20mm) so only penetrated around ⅜in (10mm) into the bowl. If they were too long I would struggle to remove the marks from the surface of the bowl.

I had turned a few square bowls/platters before, but not many. I turned the chucking tenon first, and was pleased to see it included a good portion of each quarter of the bowl, reassuring me that it would help to support the joints. I then made a few exploratory cuts to see which would produce the cleanest surface. A bevel rubbing push cut, from the centre out to the rim, worked better than a pull cut, but a shearing cut, using the wing of the

tool, with the flute closed and the handle low, produced a very fine finish and was more controllable than the push cut, especially over the corners, where bevel support was literally hit and miss.

Once I was happy with the curve I had turned, I needed to sand. I have found sanding square bowls to be hazardous at best, but with this one being so small, it was likely to be especially difficult to sand with the lathe running. I power sanded it using a 3in (75mm) arbor in my cranked drill, which is easy to use one-handed. The lathe was off and I used my left hand to hold the chuck and gently turned the lathe by hand as I worked over the surface with 240 and 320 grits, finishing by hand with 400 grit wrapped around a cork block.

Before mounting the bowl by its tenon, I finger-ruled a line around ⅜in (10mm) from the surface I had just turned. This would guide me as I turned the inside.

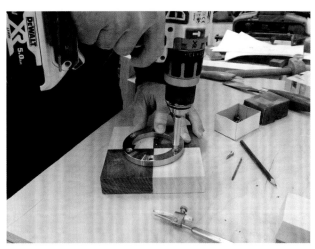
Fixing the faceplate ring for initial mounting

Using a shearing cut with my bowl gouge to produce the outer shape

Sanding the bowl

Finger-ruling the shape of the inside

TURNING THE INSIDE

With the bowl mounted in the chuck, I began to turn the inside of the bowl. This had to be done with a push cut, starting in fresh air and smoothly working into solid wood. My aim was to produce a bowl with an even edge thickness, so I needed good tool control. The line I had drawn was visible amid the blur of the edge and gave me a guide to work to.

Regular checks on progress are needed

First cuts into the bowl

Turning the centre of the bowl

I took my time as I cut into the bowl, often stopping the lathe to check my progress. I was pleased to see that there was no breakout on the edges and I was getting close to my line. I left the bulk of wood in the centre while I got the rim right as it offered stability to the blank, which was much needed with these early cuts. Only once I was satisfied that the curve of the edge was even and smooth did I move further into the bowl. Once the wings were turned, it was much more like turning a standard round bowl, but the transition between the corners and the solid wood needed to be smooth otherwise there would be a visible line or ridge where the bowl gouge suddenly finds full bevel support, so a smooth cutting action was vital.

Sanding the inside

Cutting the centre was no less important though, as the curve needed to continue right to the centre, keeping the even wall thickness throughout and avoiding any ridges or waves in the surface. Square plates and bowls are quite minimalist, so there is nowhere to hide poor turning; I took my time as I worked to the centre.

As before, I power sanded with the lathe stationary, working evenly over the surface. I made one pass under power, just over the solid part of the bowl with a 320 grit before once again turning off the lathe and hand sanding with 400 grit wrapped around a cork block.

Sanding the edges to keep them crisp

Turning the chucking tenon into a small foot

The first coat of oil goes on to the bowl

With the inside of the bowl finished, I turned my attention to the edge. There was no breakout, but the surface still showed saw cuts from when I had originally prepared the blocks of wood, so I worked through the grits from 180 to 400, again wrapped around my trusty cork block and taking great care to keep the edges crisp and not to round them over.

FINISHING

The final stage of the turning was to remove the chucking tenon and turn it into a small foot. I mounted a block of wood in the chuck and padded it out with several layers of paper towel; then I brought up the tailstock and sandwiched the bowl between the pad and the live centre. I used my ⅜in (10mm) spindle gouge to reduce the diameter of the foot and blend it into the curve of the bowl. I hand sanded to the same 400 grit

standard as the rest of the bowl and removed the bowl from the lathe. There was a tiny pip that needed sanding away from the bottom of the foot and then it was ready for an oil finish. I applied four coats of my favourite hard wax oil and gave it a gentle buff with my dome brush.

CONCLUSION

This was a roller coaster of a project, but I think the result is pretty cool! Although the original design failed, I think I could make it work, given more time and patience. Upon reflection, some of the short-grain issues could be bypassed by using long-grain jigsaw inserts, a little like butterflies or bow ties are used to stabilize cracks in wood, but more like a cartoon dog's bone, to form the jigsaw links. These could be made in a third contrasting or complementary timber.

The finished bowl

Side profile showing the pleasing curve and small foot

Star tealight holder

This project was originally made as part of a challenge to make a Christmas decoration, but it could be used as an ornament all year round. My design was inspired by some brass star-shaped candle holders that I saw online. These candles were rather tall though, which seemed a little unstable to me, so I thought a tealight in a star-shaped base would work well. Further online searches gave more inspiration. Most of the examples seemed quite small, not protruding much past the candle; I thought that, by making it larger, maybe 8in (200mm) or 10in (250mm) across, it could become a table centrepiece.

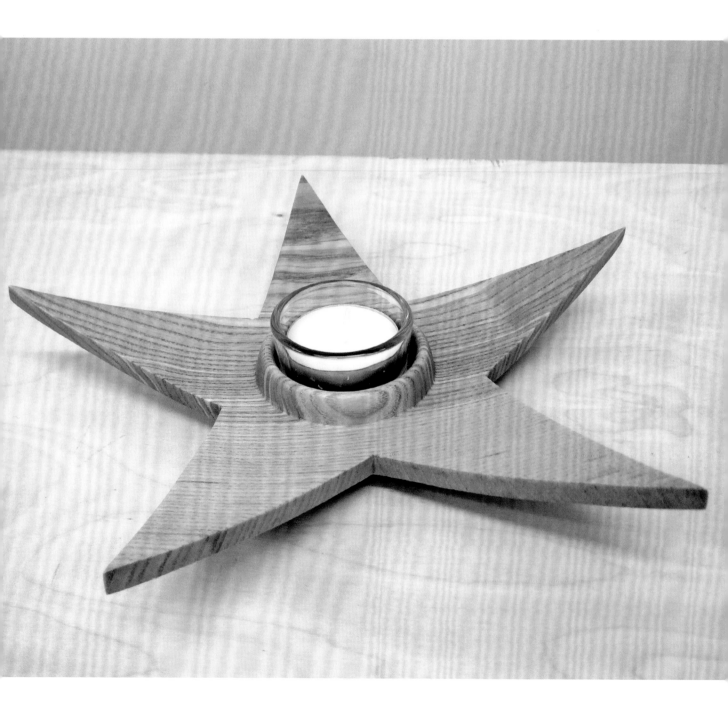

RESEARCHING TEALIGHTS

First, I needed to source some tealights. As the small candle would form the focal point of this design, I needed to make sure the star and the candle would look right proportionately together. Tealights are small, circular wax candles in a foil cup, approximately 1½in (40mm) in diameter and around ½in (12mm) tall. There has been lots of discussion and controversy in the woodturning press and online regarding the safety of placing the foil cup or candles directly into a wooden holder, and while I didn't have any solid facts either way on this matter, it seemed prudent to place the tealight inside a flameproof, heat-resistant container to minimize any fire risk. With that in mind I sourced a glass tealight holder; ceramic and metal versions are also available. The holders look good and are not particularly expensive either and with the peace of mind they give, I think it is worth using one.

STAR DESIGN

Armed with the tealights, my next task was to draw out a star. I decided on a five-point star, but how on earth should I draw it out? In times past I would have needed a specific geometry book, but now I simply looked it up on YouTube and within minutes I knew how to draw a perfect five-point star.

I first drew out the star based on a 8in (200mm) disc but it was immediately obvious that this would be too small, so I drew it again using a 10in (250mm) circle. I was much happier with this and thought a single central candle would look perfect.

I had some ash bowl blanks in stock, which were 10in (250mm) diameter and 2in (50mm) thick – just right for this job. I repeated the marking-out process for the star on one of these blanks. I was pleased with the result, although I had two main concerns. First, there was a lot of space between the five arms of the star; more than I imagined, which could make turning 'interesting', to say the least. I've turned a few square bowls and I imagined that having five points rather than four would give me a little more solid wood, but as I was working with a star rather than a solid pentagon there was actually much less wood. My second concern was that, although I know this ash turns beautifully, the open grain could cause me issues of breakout with regard to the short grain that I am likely to experience in the shape. At least one of the arms will be completely cross grain, two others will have diagonal grain – so would I suffer breakages?

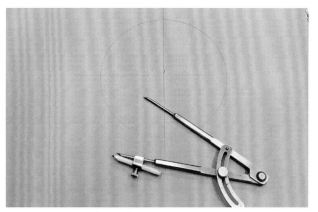
Drawing a circle with a perfect cross in the centre, the top of the vertical line will be the top of the star

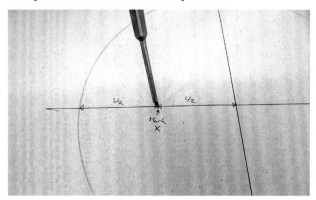
Marking the point halfway along the radius of the circle, let's call it X

Setting compasses to the distance between the top of the star and mark X

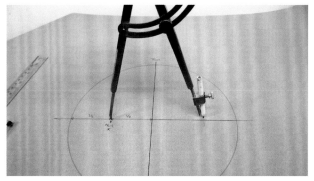
Setting the point on mark X and drawing a new mark on the same line, on the other side of the centre point

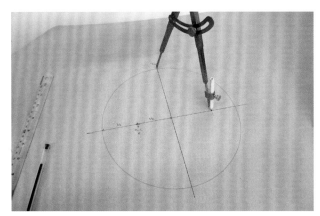
Setting the compasses to the distance between the top of the star and the new mark

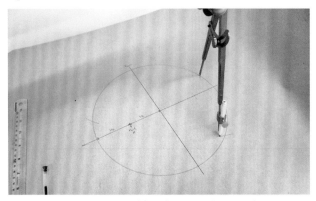
This distance should be one fifth of the circle's circumference. Marking the five points by walking the compasses around the outside of the circle

Connecting opposing marks with lines to mark out the star

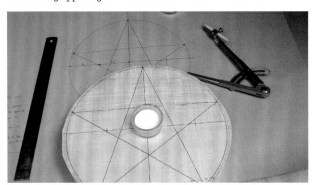
The 10in (250mm) star with a single candle looks good

TURNING

I cut the star out carefully on the bandsaw and drilled a ⁵⁄₁₆in (8mm) central hole to mount it on the screw chuck. The first thing I noticed was the huge amount of air the star moves when it's spinning on the lathe. It whirs like a propeller and I knew that great care would be needed to ensure nothing got caught in the spinning star.

The draw cut

At 2in (50mm) thick I had plenty of wood to play with, so my first job was to make a few test cuts to see if breakout was likely to be a problem. Initially I took a draw cut with the wing of my bowl gouge. In normal bowl turning this is a good cut for efficiently removing wood, but will usually not leave the best surface finish, so if breakout was going to be a problem I would find out with this cut. I was surprised to see how cleanly all but one of the arms had cut. The only area of breakout was on the top edge of the arm with grain radiating directly from the centre. I made a few more passes, this time with a push cut towards the centre. I realized that, technically, I was cutting against the grain with this cut, but it didn't hurt to gently ask questions at this point. This cut had similar results to the draw cut. I then used a push cut from the centre out to the points, which produced an improved cut with still some, but less, breakout from the same edge.

The final technique I tried was to add a light chamfer to the edge with the breakout – this is a common practice in woodwork when planing end grain, for example, to avoid breakout. I used a small, sharp chisel to slice the chamfer, then cut again. The results satisfied me that this would be the key to solving any issues that occur closer to the final cut.

As the breakout was now not such a great concern I began to shape the blank gently, keeping everything except the tool on my side of the toolrest. Initially,

The resulting breakout

Push cut with the grain

A much cleaner result

Adding a light chamfer to the edge

Fine shearing cut in action

Sanding with a cork block

Marking the toolrest to show the outer edge of the star

Finger-ruling a 5⁄16in (8mm) line

I had planned to make the star with a tall base, lifting it up from the surface it was sitting upon, but as I formed the shape I felt this would make it unstable and unsafe, so I decided to have a small foot but keep it low so that the tealight holder can't be toppled accidentally. The stability of any candle holder is of vital importance so should be the top priority when designing one.

I reduced the foot, cut a chucking tenon into it and refined the curve on the underside of the star until I was happy. To achieve the very best finish I used a fine shearing cut with the handle held low and the wing of the tool lightly slicing the wood away, regularly stopping the lathe to check my progress. I found no breakout issues, but kept my small chisel close to hand ready to slice that slight chamfer should the need arise.

There was absolutely no way this star could be safely sanded with the lathe running, so, with the lathe off, I used a cork block with abrasive wrapped around it to hand sand the underside of the star through to 400 grit.

TURNING THE INSIDE

I reversed the star on to the chuck and, before powering up the lathe, added a black mark to the toolrest to show me exactly where the extremities of the star were. My intention was to make the star with an even thickness, so I finger-ruled a line around 5⁄16in (8mm) from the pleasing curve of the underside. I repeated this on each of the star's arms and was pleased that I could clearly see the line with the lathe running. This would help guide me to an even wall thickness.

As I was essentially hollowing a shallow bowl at this point, I could only really work with a push cut towards the centre with my bowl gouge. I could see that 5⁄16in (8mm) was going to be relatively thin, especially where the cross-grain area was concerned, so I was careful to concentrate on the outer ¾–1⅛in (20–30mm) of the star to begin with, regularly checking for a smooth curve, even thickness and for breakout. I cut a slight chamfer on the one edge which showed a little breakout and that dealt with the issue perfectly.

The line is clearly visible when spinning

Turning the inside of the star

Adding the chamfer to ensure the cleanest cut

Approaching the raised area for the candle

The push cut here was the same as I would use for any bowl-turning project, but the lack of timber beneath the bevel really allowed me to see exactly what was going on. It was important to keep the bevel pointing in the direction of travel and most important to allow the wood to come to the sharp edge of the gouge without applying pressure to the wood. The arms of the star became quite flexible so too much pressure could have been disastrous. Any pressure applied with the front hand had to be downwards, into the toolrest as support and not into the wood.

Once the outer ¾–1⅛in (20–30mm) was turned to my satisfaction and I moved further into the bowl, I couldn't return to the outer edge as vibration would be an issue and I wouldn't be able to support the wood with my fingers as I would on a normal thin bowl.

As I began to approach the centre of the star I knew that I needed to allow a space for the tealight holder. There were a few options open to me but I liked the idea of a beaded detail to hold the tealight holder, which

would also hide some of the foil cup, which I don't find particularly attractive.

I measured and marked a 1¾in (45mm) diameter area in the centre for the glass cup and hollowed it out using a spindle gouge, cutting on the lower wing as I would if I were hollowing a box. Technically this isn't the correct cut for a cross-grain 'bowl blank' like this, but it efficiently and safely removed the excess wood, so there was no issue. I used my ⅜in (10mm) round negative rake scraper to properly flatten the inside of this recess cleanly before using a ¼in (6mm) bead-forming tool to produce a rounded top. As I continued to shape the area it became clear that, although in my head the detail was going to be a simple bead, it actually needed to stand a fair bit higher than just the ¼in (6mm) bead, so I could have simply turned it with a gouge. That said, it was a simple way to do it.

After tidying up the area where the wings of the star meet the raised central area for the candle with careful cuts with my spindle gouge, which I feel more

Scraping the inside of the candle cup area

Careful hand sanding of the candle cup

Sanding the arms with the cork block

Power sanding the edges

comfortable using in tight spaces, it was time to sand. I could safely sand the central candle area and just outside of it with the lathe spinning, but, like on the outside, I had no other option but to hand sand the face of the star. I had to be incredibly careful with this stage as there was visible flex on each of the arms and I was extra cautious when it came to the arm with the short grain. Despite the flex, I suffered no breakages as I sanded from 180 to 400 grit.

THE EDGES

With both faces sanded smooth I needed to address the edges of the star that were still showing the rough cuts from the bandsaw. I had mused on dealing with these before I turned it but had decided that I would be wasting my time and effort as most of the wood would end up on the floor. There's little point smoothing 2in (50mm)-wide wood when I actually only need ⁵⁄₁₆in (8mm) of smooth wood. The only issue was that now the arms were more delicate. I had thought about using a cabinet scraper, which would produce a beautifully smooth surface with little care for the grain direction. However, with such short

grain I thought I would be risking breaking off the points of at least two, but possibly more, of the arms. I looked again at my razor-sharp little chisel but grain direction would cause some issues with this option. Sanding seemed to be the way forward, but hand sanding wouldn't be much fun, so I opted for power sanding.

I put a fresh 2in (50mm) disc of 240 grit on to the arbor in my cranked drill and gently tried it out on one of the better-supported arms and it worked perfectly. My cranked drill was quite expensive to buy compared to a standard drill, but I wouldn't be without it now. I don't think I've ever actually drilled a hole with it, but as a sanding tool it is second to none. Easily handled and controllable with one hand while the other supports the work, it made light work of smoothing the edges of the star.

I spend a few minutes afterwards tidying up the corners with my little chisel and then hand sanded through to 400 grit so all surfaces were equally sanded and the sharp edges were softened slightly.

Reversing the star

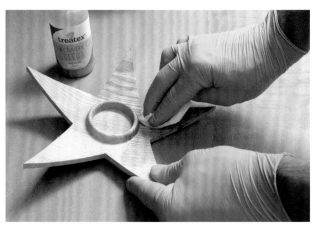
Oiling the star

REVERSING THE STAR

For most reverse faceplate work, I have a disc of MDF permanently mounted on to a faceplate and I sandwich the work between this disc and the live centre. In the past, I have tried placing various means of padding between the work and the MDF disc but they all seem to leave more of a mark than using nothing at all, so I no longer bother. The disc is around 14in (350mm) in diameter so I can reverse most types of work over it; however, in this case it would be of no use because only the five tips of the star would touch it and as soon as I applied pressure with the tailstock it would almost certainly snap the star across the short grain.

Looking at the star, the rounded edge of the candle centre would sit against a flat surface to allow me to drive it, so I placed a small disc of ply on to my screw chuck and brought up the live centre. It worked perfectly, keeping the arms of the star well out of harm's way while I turned the chucking tenon away, refined the foot and sanded it all to 400 grit.

The tiny pip that remained from the live centre was power sanded away using the abrasive pad in my cranked drill. I applied four coats of my favourite satin hard wax oil as a finish.

CONCLUSION

I imagine a non-turner looking at this might assume it to be a simple little project, but there is considerable tool control required to produce the smooth, even, curving surfaces of the star. A closer-grained timber would probably be more stable and less likely to break along the grain and, although I got away with it here, I don't feel like it would survive being dropped or banged around too much.

SAFETY NOTE

After the original article about this project was published, I received a few comments that it was unsafe and that I should have turned a circular bowl and cut the star from it instead. I thought I would take this opportunity to address these comments. This is undoubtedly an advanced turning project and the whole concept of the series of articles was to challenge me, as a professional turner. As with anything in turning, if you don't feel comfortable making this, please do not attempt it. If you are confident in your ability to turn precisely, can make very controlled cuts, have a full understanding of safe practices on a lathe and have successfully made several square bowls, then there is no reason you can't have a go at this project.

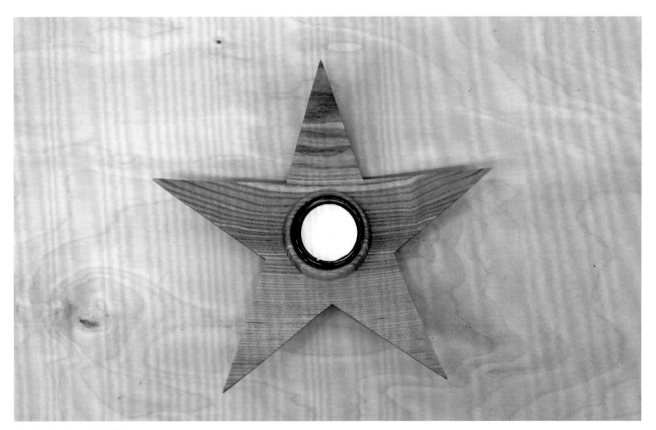

The finished candle holder

Ebonized and fumed bowl

This project was part of a challenge on using traditional wood colouring techniques, specifically the traditional processes of ebonizing and fuming. I was aware of both techniques and had read about their use, but I had never actually tried either of them. I was keen to have a go and planned to make a bowl incorporating both ebonizing and fuming, but first I needed to do some research on the materials and processes involved, and then carry out some experiments.

RESEARCH ON EBONIZING

Ebonizing solution is a mix of acetic acid and iron which, when applied to a wood with a tannin content, turns the wood black. At the mention of acid most people (including me) get a little nervous, but acetic acid is actually no more exotic than the standard vinegar you might add to your fish and chips, and the iron can come from anything with an iron content, including steel items such as screws, nails and steel wool.

I read a number of online articles and forum discussions about it. While there are several slightly differing opinions about the exact approach, there is a general consensus that any vinegar can be used as a base liquid for the solution. I read a number of discussions about whether rusty screws and nails are needed – many seem to think they are, but it seems clean steel wool can be used as long as there isn't too much oil in it. Some wash it first but I know good quality '0000' steel wool used by furniture restorers is very fine (so should dissolve quite quickly) and very clean, so as not to make a mess of antique furniture.

I was slightly concerned about the length of time the steel wool might need to sit in the vinegar, but most people suggest a couple of weeks should be enough.

EBONIZING EXPERIMENTS

My first stop was my local supermarket to buy vinegar. I had no idea there would be so many options. Armed with the knowledge that any vinegar could do the job I looked for the cheapest and found a choice of malt vinegar, which is the familiar brown liquid I would add to chips, or a clear version called distilled vinegar. I thought a clear liquid would make it easier to monitor the progress of the chemical reaction, so I chose that one. On the way back to the workshop I called into my local tool and hardware shop to pick up a small pack of good quality '0000' steel wool.

I always keep a few glass jars at the workshop – you just never know when they'll come in handy. An old mayo jar with a screw-down lid should be ideal here. I wasn't certain about correct quantities or ratios so I tore off some steel wool and put it in the jar until it looked a bit over half full, then poured the vinegar over it until the jar was mostly full. Not very scientific, but I hoped it would work.

I drilled a ⅛in (3mm) hole in the lid of the jar. Before my research I hadn't realized that the chemical reaction produces a certain amount of gas, which needs to escape,

Distilled vinegar and steel wool to make the ebonizing solution

Adding the vinegar to the steel wool

The re-labelled jar with the fresh solution

Filtering the solution ...

... still murky but now with no bits

The remnant of steel wool

The tea experiment with freshly applied ebonizing solution

After 15 minutes there is no difference between them

so this small hole should do the trick. I gave the jar a good shake (with my finger over the hole) and put it to one side to do its thing. I also re-labelled the jar to make it clear what was inside, which is a sensible precaution. I then left the solution for two and a half weeks, giving the jar a good shake nearly every day.

When the time was up, there was a layer of rust at the top of the liquid and it looked decidedly murky. I decided to run the liquid through a paint strainer before applying it to any wood. I selected another jar and filtered into it. The new liquid was still murky, but at least there were no bits floating in it. The remnant of the steel wool left in the original jar showed just how much had dissolved, which I took as an encouraging sign. I think it would have completely dissolved in another two weeks.

My research had thrown up an interesting piece of information about ebonizing: this method of colouring wood works best on wet, or at least partially seasoned, wood. All the wood in my workshop is prime furniture grade, seasoned timber, so I wondered if this would be a problem. One solution to this, apparently, is to apply a coat of strong tea to the wood before adding the vinegar and steel mix. Tea is full of tannin, so presumably adds to the effect.

I decided to give this a go. I used masking tape on an oak offcut to give me four sections to play with. The article I'd read about the tea hadn't gone into much detail about it, other than to say it should be strong. Should I let it dry? Should it be wet when I applied the ebonizing solution? I didn't know, so I decided to leave one square bare as a reference, use just the ebonizing solution on one, and apply tea to the other two, but leave one wet and dab the other dry.

I made a strong cup of tea using five standard teabags. After letting it mash and cool for a while, I spread tea on two of the squares with a paintbrush and after a couple of minutes I dabbed one dry using a paper towel. I then painted on the ebonizing solution, starting with the bare wood square.

Each of the quadrants began to darken quickly but the wet tea section went a deeper colour much faster than the others, followed by the dry tea section and finally the bare part. It seemed that the tea did have an effect, but within 15 minutes of applying the vinegar mix, all three sections were the same deep blue/black colour, with hardly any difference between them.

Obviously this was just one experiment on one piece of wood, which is hardly scientific, as the most accurate results will always come from a much larger controlled experiment. But it seemed that my ebonizing solution worked perfectly well on kiln-dried European oak and the addition of strong tea made no difference to the end result.

RESEARCH ON FUMING

This seems to be a less complex process, but also involves a chemical reaction between the natural tannins in some types of wood and the gases that come from ammonia. The fuming process was first discovered when it was noticed that oak boards stored in a stable darkened, caused by the fumes from naturally occurring ammonia in horse urine. Experiments proved it to be a great way of speeding up the natural darkening of some woods – particularly oak.

There are two main types of ammonia – a strong industrial version used on a bigger, industrial scale, or household ammonia, which is effectively a cleaning product. For my purposes, where accessibility and safety are important, the household version was

more appropriate. Ammonia is not readily available in supermarkets but I found some in a local independent hardware store. Like the vinegar and steel wool, the ammonia had a very low cost, meaning these techniques promised to be some of the cheapest methods I had ever used to colour wood.

HEALTH AND SAFETY

The innocuous sounding name 'household ammonia' on the front of the bottle is in stark contrast to the back, where the list of hazard warnings is quite alarming. Reading the instructions, when mixed into water (importantly, not the other way around) it is used at about a 50:1 ratio of water to ammonia, but straight from the bottle it can severely burn skin and eyes. Its vapour damages lungs and immediate medical advice must be sought should any be swallowed. Throughout this process, when I handled ammonia I wore long sleeves, protective gloves, an FFA1P2-rated spray mask, eye protection and worked in a well ventilated area (outside) just to be on the safe side.

Household ammonia

Safety warnings on the ammonia

FUMING EXPERIMENTS

Both these colouring techniques are best known for working on oak, but I was curious to see if they would do anything to other woods. I've seen fuming done before using a thick plastic dust extractor bag, but during my online research I saw a description of using a plastic stacking box with a locking lid for fuming small items. Having some of those in regular use in the workshop, this seemed ideal.

I decided to begin with an experiment. I knew that oak would show some sort of reaction, but I wasn't sure about other woods. I cut sample pieces, around 4in (100mm) long, from the woods I had lying around in the workshop: oak, ash, steamed beech, sapele, sycamore, American black walnut and iroko.

I carefully poured some ammonia into a glass jar and placed it into the storage box, along with samples of the different woods, which I placed on another piece of wood to allow the fumes to circulate. I guessed the part of the wood sitting on the base board wouldn't change colour.

After 24 hours I took the sealed box outside and carefully opened the lid to allow the fumes to dissipate. When it was safe, I took a look inside. Each piece of timber looked slightly 'aged' but the oak was the only one with a significant colour change – it now looked closer to the walnut sample than to the original piece of oak. As predicted, the back of the samples had not changed colour. This confirmed that oak would be the best choice for my bowl.

The wood samples ready for fuming

Laid out in the box with the jar of ammonia

Left to fume for 24 hours in the sealed box

The oak has the most colour change

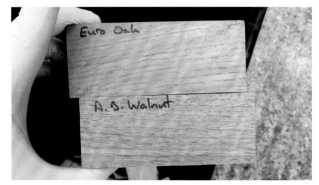

The fumed oak is closer to the colour of walnut

Even the beech has changed colour a little, looking slightly more aged

Turning the oak bowl

Applying the ebonizing solution

Allowing it to work

Slight colouring on the back of the edge sands off easily

TURNING THE BOWL

I had proved that both techniques worked well on European oak so I selected a piece of 2in (50mm)-thick quartersawn oak and decided to make a wide-rimmed bowl to one of my favourite shapes. I turned an ogee-shaped underside with a broad foot. The top rim had a gentle curve with a small fillet, giving a sharp contrast to the sweeping and slightly undercut bowl.

Before turning the inside, I applied the ebonizing solution to the rim with a paintbrush. At this point the bowl was still fixed in the chuck and both were removed from the lathe together to allow me to paint on the solution flat on the bench. Initially it turned a dark brown, and within minutes a deep black with a slight blue hint to it. I dabbed off the excess solution and left it overnight to fully dry.

The following morning, I replaced the bowl on the lathe, checking it was still firmly gripped by the chuck. Despite my careful application of the ebonizing solution, there were some slight brush marks on the edge of the underside. I hoped I could sand these away and was relieved to find that was the case, so I re-sanded the underside from 180 to 400 grit to ensure it was all clean. I was then able to turn the inside of the bowl and sand to match the rest. I carefully remounted the bowl and removed the chucking tenon, sanding the base of the foot smooth and to the same standard as the rest of the bowl.

At this point the contrast between the pale oak and the ebonized rim looked great. I'm not generally a huge fan of coloured work, but where a detail like this adds a contrast I do like it. I was aware that by fuming it

Turning the inside

The finished bowl before fuming

Bowl in the fuming box

Fresh from the fuming box

The underside with the light oak base

Applying oil

the contrast would be reduced somewhat as the oak darkened to deeper shade, but I was certain that contrast would still be effective.

It occurred to me at this point that I was not sure exactly what would happen to the ebonized portion in the fuming box. I guessed it would only get darker, if any change happened at all, but I would find out soon enough.
I placed a flat disc of wood on the floor of the box and sat the oak bowl on it. My aim was for the bottom of the foot to remain light oak in colour as a surprising contrast to anyone (presumably a woodturner) who might turn it over to take a look at the base. I poured a similar amount of fresh ammonia into the same jar as before and shut down the lid of the box for 24 hours.

THE BIG REVEAL
I was excited to see how it looked when it came out of the box. As before, I took it outside to allow the fumes to dissipate harmlessly, and carefully opened the lid. Two things immediately struck me. First, the darkness

of the oak. Seeing a small sample is one thing but when you see the effect on a finished piece it has so much more impact. The advantage of fuming over staining became obvious too, as the colour was even no matter what the grain direction, whereas with a stain, the end grain will always absorb more and be darker. Second, the ebonized rim was something of a surprise because, rather than the blue/black it had been when it went in to the fume box, it was now an incredibly deep, rich, dark brown. Applying three coats of hard wax oil and a gentle buff only brought out the richness of the colours further.

CONCLUSION
I was pleased with the outcome of the bowl and found it fascinating to see how using a combination of essentially everyday items could produce such dramatic results. There was nothing new in what I'd done – these are very traditional techniques after all – but having these techniques in my armoury of ways to change the appearance of wood could be very useful in the future.

The finished bowl

Airbrushed fire bowl

Although I had owned an airbrush kit for a few years, I had never done anything more than play with it until this challenge was issued. My task was to decorate a turned item; as well as being a novice with an airbrush, I don't have a lot of artistic skills, so it took me a while to decide on a design that I thought I could achieve successfully. I eventually settled on a fire theme for this bowl. Flames are abstract enough that there isn't a definite right or wrong to them, making them more achievable for an airbrushing beginner like me.

RESEARCH

Using the tool itself was reasonably straightforward, but making it do something other than 'colouring in' was where the challenge really lay. I turned to YouTube to see if I could get some guidance and ideas. I found a good video in which the demonstrator talked through the basic equipment and showed some useful exercises to practise trigger control. I found several other videos which all described the process. They varied slightly but the core of the information was largely the same.

Next, I looked online for airbrush paint. There were lots of different options and, to be honest, I didn't really know where to start. I decided to speak to one of my usual finishes suppliers and so emailed my friends at Chestnut Products. They explained that they do a couple of different paint products that can work with an airbrush, although they need to thinned slightly to work properly. They agreed to send me some samples over to try out.

I received a sample pack of metallic paints and iridescent paints, along with a bottle of airbrush cleaner and a reducer to thin down the paint. I've done quite a bit of spray finishing in the past so I felt reasonably confident that I could achieve the correct consistency to spray through the airbrush. Actual airbrush paints are usually supplied ready to put straight into the airbrush.

My airbrush kit with compressor and airbrush

The paints, reducer and airbrush cleaner from Chestnut Products

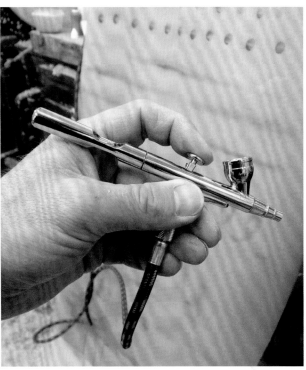

The airbrush fits the hand well

PRACTISING AIRBRUSHING

The airbrush is a well-designed little tool. It fits the hand comfortably (whether you are right or left-handed) and the trigger mechanism is a two-stage operation. When the trigger is pushed down, air flows through the airbrush, but doesn't add the paint. It is important to keep the air flowing all the time to achieve smooth lines and fine control. Once the trigger is pulled back the paint begins to be sprayed; the further the trigger is pulled back, the more paint is applied. With practice and good finger control, this allows variation from a solid line to a very light shading to be applied.

The small paint pot at the top of the airbrush means that it is quite simple to change the paint to another colour. There are different styles of airbrush which allow a bottle of paint to be fitted and easily swapped to another colour, although these seem to be a more 'professional' option.

I began with some exercises, as recommended in the video online. I leant a sheet of ply against my lathe and used masking tape to fix a sheet of brown craft paper to it, forming a rudimentary easel. Knowing that I will need red, yellow and white for the fire on my bowl, I kept those colours safely off to one side and started with green. First, I made a series of dots, a good exercise to practise trigger control by making a line of the same sized dots, first small, then slightly larger.

Practising my exercises

The second exercise was to draw a line which went from thick to thin and back again. As before, getting this right was all about trigger control. I then practised smooth movements by making a continuous row of 'e's, which reminded me of primary school, but again was good control practice. I used up three sheets with these exercises and finished by signing my name at the bottom!

Signing my first work of art

FIRE STENCIL TEMPLATE

Feeling increasingly confident, I decided to have a go at painting some fire. The videos I had watched all described using some sort of stencil template to give a little definition to the flames. I've seen stencils used with huge success by artists such as Nick Agar, who has used everything from leaves to sprockets to add flavour to his work. While the technique for fire is similar, I didn't need a complete flame stencil (although I could if I wanted a more cartoon-like fire effect), but more a curve stencil, which allows for a stronger edge here and there and helps to achieve a fantastic natural fire effect – at least it did when someone skilled with an airbrush did it.

In the video I watched, the guy had cut out a kind of cloverleaf shape, with each of the round shapes being different diameters, allowing him to achieve different, yet controlled, curves. I cut out a similar template from a sheet of thick paper. I made mine much smaller though as my fire would be smaller than the one in the video.

Aware that the sample bottles of paint I had were not very big, I stuck with green for the first layer of my practice. I used largely upward strokes, adding my template in random places (which was much more difficult than it sounds), varying which curve I used. I tried to copy the demonstrator in the video and add more weight behind the hard edge of the stencil curve and fade it out. I then randomly picked another colour, which happened to be purple, and added the second layer of colour. The video suggested around six layers are best to achieve real depth to the fire. After the purple, I could see where I should be aiming, but with the colours being so far from those of an actual fire, it was difficult to visualize, so I picked three colours closer to red, yellow and white. I chose copper, gold and pink for the next test. This allowed me to layer the paint better and gave me a much clearer idea of how it would look.

While the result was still a million miles from the videos I had watched, I was encouraged that things were moving in the right direction and that there was at least a suggestion of flames, even if they lacked the realism I would ideally love to achieve.

I decided it was time for a practice run that would more closely simulate the final product: a small, wide-rimmed bowl in a light wood. I planned to spray the rim black

Clover-shaped stencil template

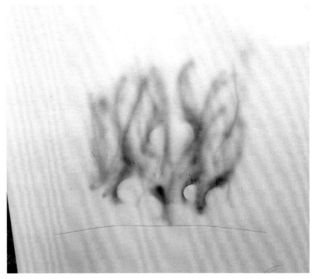

My first attempt was in the wrong colour but showed hints of fire

Using the stencil to give random definition

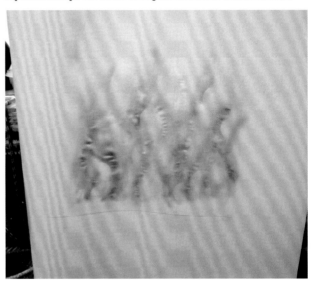

Second attempt was an improvement but still lots to learn

Thinning the paint

The paint ready to spray

and add the fire before hollowing a small bowl from the centre. The way I saw it in my mind, the fire would radiate from the centre, rather than from an imaginary source outside of the bowl.

I cut a 8in (200mm) disc of thick paper and thinned down a little of each of my three colours with the reducer. My earlier experiments showed that I only needed to add a few drops of reducer to achieve a sprayable medium. In preparation I had bought some lidded containers, in which I could mix the paints thoroughly with lollipop sticks and add the lids until I needed each colour.

FINAL PRACTICE
The beauty of painting a big sheet of paper is that a really fluid, long, licking flame can be produced, but I was very aware that on a 8in (200mm) disc I would need to achieve the same effect but in a far more compact way. I began with red and immediately realized that the iridescent red in the Chestnut sample pack was actually quite pink, so I added a little black to it. I know from my restoration work that black tones down red, for example if a mahogany stain is too red then a few drops of black can take it to where it needs to be.

I used the template curves randomly around the disc and I added shading and weight to the lines. I followed up with yellow, then more red, some white, yellow, red and white, just as recommended on the videos.

The result was ... shall I say, interesting? It wasn't quite what I wanted, looking far more like an accident in a paint factory than a blazing inferno, but I had learned a huge amount from it. There was too much red and not enough layering, so I probably used too much red too early. I just needed a little more restraint. On the positive side, the colours were good and there were definitely some areas that screamed 'fire' at me. If I couldn't achieve realism (which would be difficult with only a few hours of practice), then I at least wanted it to be easily recognizable as fire. I also felt that, once applied to a solid black background rather than to cream paper, then the flames would look far better.

THE BOWL
I rummaged through one of my timber stacks and found a board of light-coloured beech, around 2in (50mm) thick, which looked suitable for the bowl. I could make an 8in (200mm) bowl from it, which was roughly what I had in mind.

I mounted it on a screw chuck, trued it up and turned the underside into a simple, fluid ogee shape, which I always prefer on wide-rimmed bowls. I sanded to 400 grit and re-chucked the bowl to shape the top. I turned the gentlest of curves across the surface. Too much of a curve on this type of bowl can make it look like it's drooping, which isn't a good look, but likewise dead flat isn't interesting either, so it is a fine balance to strike. Once I was happy, I sanded to the same 400 grit as the underside and applied a light spray of sanding sealer. After about half an hour I lightly cut the surface back with a fine abrasive pad and took it to my spray booth to apply a coat of ebonizing lacquer. After a couple of hours, I lightly cut it back with 600-grit abrasive and re-coated it, leaving it overnight to fully cure before I began the airbrushing work.

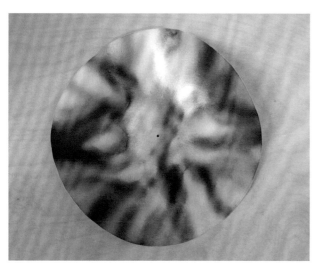

The final fire practice

Certain areas show promise

Shaping the top face of the bowl

Beginning to turn the top surface after turning the underside

Spraying the first coat of ebonizing lacquer

Applying red and using the stencil template

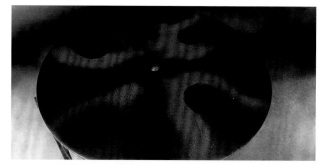

The first red flames in place

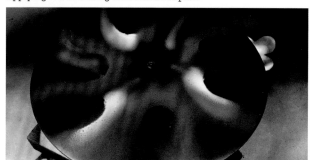

Yellow subdues the red and white adds highlights

Making orange by adding red to yellow

The orange is really effective

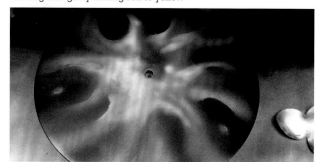

More white 'hot' highlights are added

Quick strokes of yellow add real life to it

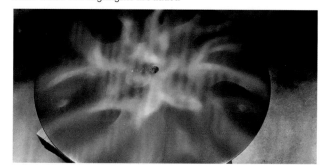

A little more red and it is time to stop

Turning the tiny bowl

Satin lacquer completes the job

HEALTH AND SAFETY

I used water-based paints, which don't have the strong chemical smell of most lacquers; however, after I had been spraying them through the airbrush for some time I could feel the overspray in the air on my chest. I realized I should have worn a spray mask but foolishly, because I was only doing small work, I hadn't bothered. I really should know better by now. As I carried the bowl upstairs to my small spray booth to spray it black, I had a realization that I should have done all of this spraying in the booth. The rest of this project was done in the spray booth and I wore my spray mask. This is a reminder that even for a small amount of work like this, good ventilation and a suitable protective mask are needed.

FINAL AIRBRUSHING

Naturally, I felt a certain amount of pressure to get this right. I tried to remind myself that if it looked terrible, I could lightly sand it back, re-spray it with black and start again, with nothing lost but time. It was important to relax – tension and stress are poor companions when trying to achieve your best work.

I started with red, spraying around the template and trying to achieve natural, flowing curves. The second coat was yellow, sprayed lightly over the red. Third was a new series of strokes in white. Between each colour change, I ran airbrush cleaner through the tool and thoroughly cleaned it with paper towel to minimize colour contamination.

I felt that there was a lot of wet paint on it at this point so stepped away for half an hour to let it dry, then went back to it with fresh eyes to re-evaluate it. I could definitely see the beginnings of something but it was hard to know if it was right at this point.

When I'd watched the videos, I'd made notes about which colours were used and when. Looking at my work so far, I felt something was missing. I looked at my notes and saw orange on the list. I didn't have an orange, but I did have yellow and red – surely yellow with a few drops of red would create orange? I reached for the last unused lidded box and mixed it up. The result was a vibrant orange which, when sprayed on some white paper towel, looked very promising. I worked over the flames I'd painted so far, this time not using the template, but highlighting some of the flames as naturally as possible. This is what had been missing and it definitely had more of a fire look to it now.

Next, I added some white to highlight the hotspots of the flame. Once again, I left it for a while to dry. I really didn't want to rush and spoil it at this point.

The centre area was still a bit of a mess but I wasn't worried as this would be cut away – I just wasn't sure yet exactly how big the bowl in the centre would be, but I didn't expect to be able to fit much into it.

Next, I added some quick but definite strokes of yellow. The final colour was more red, just to calm those yellows a little. It would be so easy just to keep going, but I felt now was the point to stop. I hoped I had done enough to convey the idea of fire. I left it for a few hours to dry before taking it back to the lathe.

Re-mounting in the chuck was no problem and I studied the flame design to try to ensure that I removed the area in the centre, which was mostly a blob of colourful paint, but did not remove any of the base of the fire. I scored a line with the tip of my skew, cautiously small, and stopped the lathe to check. I increased it slightly and, satisfied, I continued to hollow the tiny bowl, which was only about 2¾in (70mm) across, adding a slight undercut for further interest. Throughout this process I was incredibly careful of the paintwork because, although it was touch dry, it hadn't fully cured, due to the number of layers involved.

To finish, I removed the tenon to leave a flat base and, in the spray booth, applied a couple of light coats of satin acrylic lacquer.

CONCLUSION

Despite my early reservations (painted work is not really my thing), I enjoyed learning the airbrushing technique. The Chestnut paints worked really well, although I think the correct opaque airbrush paints may have given a more realistic fire, especially in the hands of a more competent airbrush artist. The paints I used were metallic, so my fire has a sparkly quality, which I don't mind at all. I am pleased with the finished bowl and, considering this is only my fourth attempt at fire (two on brown paper, one on a disc of cream paper and this one), I am feeling very pleased with myself. The internet, used correctly, is such a fantastic tool for learning and without it I would have struggled so much with many of these challenges.

Basketweave illusion bowl

The basketweave illusion technique has grown in popularity in recent years, especially in the US, where the designs are often inspired by traditional Native American basketwork. Usually, basketweave illusion patterns are added to bowls, platters or hollow forms made from pale-coloured woods, which allows for the burning and colouring details to stand out. Rows of beads are cut into the surface of the piece, then divided up into little squares with pyrography and coloured in to form a colourful, grid-like pattern, which resembles the elaborate weaving of a basket. My challenge was to incorporate basketweave in a turning. Rather than covering a whole piece, I came up with this semi-enclosed bowl featuring a band of a basketweave illusion design.

DESIGN

My first job was to find a suitable piece of timber. I was originally asked to make a deep bowl as a canvas for this project and as I sorted through my timber pile I found a piece of 4in (100mm) sapele that looked promising. The main issue with sapele, though, is that it is a deep red/brown colour and not the usual pale timber used for this type of work. This set my brain ticking. Could I use a darker wood and still pull off a basketweave illusion? Mulling over the problem, I kept thinking about the colour of the sapele and couldn't help thinking that an enclosed bowl-type design in this red/brown wood might look a little like terracotta ... Once this thought occurred there was no stopping me.

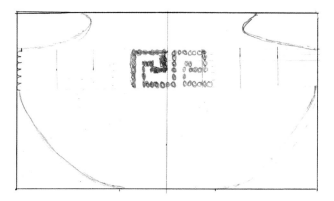

Initial sketch

What if my inspiration wasn't from North America, but somewhere else in the world? My mind went on a metaphorical journey through southern Europe and somehow ended up with an Ancient Greek-inspired terracotta vase, which should naturally have a Greek-inspired pattern running in a band around it in a Greek key design.

I drew out a square on paper around 7¼in (185mm) across and 4in (100mm) deep, and sketched out a shape to fit inside it. I should say that the shape I came up with is my perception of a Greek-inspired vase, rather than based on anything specific.

GREEK KEY MOTIF

Satisfied with the shape of the bowl, I needed to research the Greek key design. It didn't take too much searching on the internet to find a version made up of little squares, a little like mosaic tiles, which was perfect, as it allowed me to really get to grips with the shape of the repeating pattern.

Based on this tile pattern, I needed a grid made up of seven tiles – or, in this case, beads – high. The pattern repeats itself every eight squares, so I needed an index division number which is divisible by 8. My indexing plate has a 60-hole setting as standard, so with a little adjustment in the locking arm I was able to easily double this and achieve 120 positions, which conveniently divides by eight, giving me 15 repeats of the pattern around the bowl.

I needed to cut regular beads, which of course could be done freehand, but is more easily achieved with a beading tool. I have a ¼in (6mm) tool, but that would be too big for this job. I also have a Crown fluted parting tool which, because of its design, can be used as a makeshift beading tool, cutting a ⅛in (4mm)-wide bead.

A little simple maths proves that using 120 index stops should leave me with pretty much ⅛in (4mm) squares, which should be very effective.

To fix the design in my mind I drew it out full size on a grid, 7 squares deep and 24 squares long, allowing me to colour in 3 repeats of the design. This would be a valuable reference in setting out the pattern later.

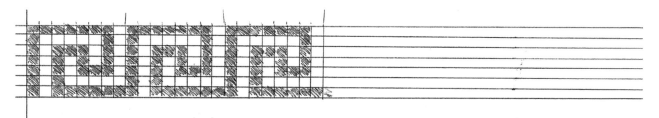

Layout of the Greek key design

TURNING

I spent an enjoyable hour or so turning the bowl, using a combination of bowl gouges, a cranked hollowing tool and a negative rake scraper. I decided this doesn't need to be particularly thin. As it was intended to be representative of terracotta, I felt a bit of weight should work well, so finished it to a pleasingly regular ⅜in (10mm) wall thickness. Being able to turn a shape from my imagination rather than something prescribed by a customer is always a liberating and satisfying experience for me and this shape is one I had never made before so presented its own challenges, especially in the undercut.

Fluted parting tool in action

Turning the bowl

Close-up of the tool

BEADING

Having fully turned and sanded the vase to 320 grit, I was ready to cut the beads. I sharpened the fluted parting tool by touching the front bevel to the grinder and marked out roughly where I wanted the beads to be. There was a slight curve to the surface as the shape seemed to flow better like this. I presented the tool perpendicular to the bowl as I work around the slight curve. I experimented a little with the presentation of the tool to get the best cut and was pleased to find no chipping or tear-out, which can sometimes happen with beading tools. Satisfied with the beads, I lightly sanded them to ensure they were smooth.

From my research, I learned that the lines between each bead are usually burned with a piece of laminate, sometimes referred to by the brand name Formica. I had a piece of this which was given to me by a friend some time ago, but I had never actually used it, so this was a good place to start. It seemed a little thick compared to the gaps between the beads so I took it to my little disc sander and tapered the faces a little, producing a thinner edge.

I kept the toolrest in place to stabilize my hands and the laminate and gently pushed it into the groove between

Refining the edge of the laminate on my disc sander

Using the laminate on the bowl

the beads. It certainly defined the line better than just using the parting tool, but I was a little disappointed that it didn't produce the dark line I've seen on other work, even at top speed. In this case, I could have used a thin wire burner to highlight the lines but, as I don't have one, I settled for the result and moved on.

PYROGRAPHY

I was supplied with a pyrography machine and a selection of tips to try out. The machine is a Razortip SK unit, made in Canada and available worldwide. The Razortip brochure shows a mind-boggling range of around 850 different tip variations for creating all sorts of different burning and branding effects. It seems pyrography is a whole other rabbit hole in which to get lost!

My main research for this part of the process was watching a YouTube video of a demonstration by Doug Schneiter, a very talented specialist in the field (www. youtube.com/watch?v=FKMpLUpoiKg). In the video, Doug explains that there are two main methods to score the dividing lines into the rows of beads. Burning the lines produces the required grid effect and has the added bonus of acting like a dam to stop the colour from

The two most suitable pyro pen tips for this job

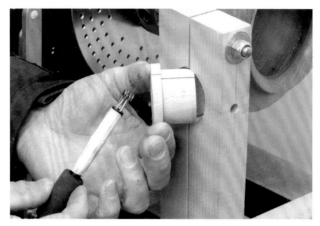
The adaptor I turned to allow the pyro pen to fit in the router jig

The pen held in place

The business end of the pen

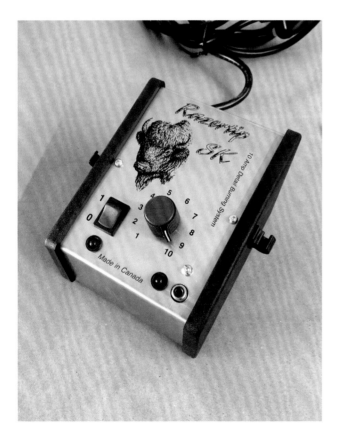
The pyrography unit used

bleeding. His preferred method is to draw lines on the work with a pencil, using a platform to rest the pencil on and an indexer to lock the work in position. He then uses a skewed knife-shaped tip and freehand burns the lines into the work. Not confident I could do this to a high standard on my first attempt, I took his second suggestion, which is to use a special U-shaped tip that closely matched the beads I had turned, and burn the lines one by one, either freehand or using a jig. A couple of pictures I'd seen during my research had shown the pyro pen held level with the bed at centre height on a jig or platform and then applied to the work in a very controlled way. Seeing this I immediately knew what I should do: I could easily adapt my router jig to hold the pyro pen.

My router jig is a simple L-shaped jig which holds the router horizontally on centre height, and is lightly held to the lathe bed by a T-nut. A slot in the base allows good side-to-side and front-to-back movement. Where the router is usually held, I added a simple turned collar which allowed the jig to grip the smaller pyro pen. I added a little masking tape to the pen to aid the grip. I fixed the indexing jig to the lathe and was ready to burn.

BURNING

In the video, Doug suggests setting 5 on the pyrography machine he used for his method, which seems a good place to start, setting 1 being the coolest and 10 being the hottest. After leaving it for a few minutes to warm up I applied the tool to the wood and, to my dismay, nothing happened. I turned it up to 6 and tried again, leaving it against the wood for longer. This time I could see that it was working but not as planned. The shape of the pyro tip was similar, but crucially not the same as the bead I had cut, so it was only burning the very outsides of the bead and not the middle. A rethink was in order. Maybe Doug's technique would be better?

I remembered being told these Razortip units are more powerful than some and are capable of some quite deep branding and it occurred to me that this was exactly what I needed to do – deeply brand the bead. If I could get the tip hot enough it should burn the shape of the tip into the bead and it shouldn't matter that they don't match exactly. I cranked the unit up to 10 and almost immediately the tip began to glow literally red hot. Applying the tip this time was much more dramatic as a small plume of smoke rose from the contact area. I had the result I was after. Now I just needed to repeat this across the seven beads and then 120 times around the bowl ... yes, 840 individual burns.

My first attempt at burning didn't go to plan

Glowing red hot, I have much more success

The first 60 lines are finished

Adjusting the indexing jig

Making sure the spacing is good before continuing

With the burning complete

It took around 90 minutes to complete the first set of 60 and I was pleased with the look of it. I checked over my work and touched up a couple of lines which weren't quite as dark as I'd like. The spacing was around ⅜in (10mm), so as long as I could get my adjustment of the indexer right, I should end up with good, even squares once I repeated the process.

I carefully marked the halfway point between the first set of burn lines and adjusted the vertical arm of the indexing mechanism. The design of the jig made this easy to do and I was more than satisfied with the new setting. I then simply repeated the process. It was slow going and I can see that some people would find it incredibly tedious, others perhaps quite relaxing. Either way, the end result was very pleasing and, I thought, worth the time and effort. The burn pattern looked quite effective on its own, even before the colour was added, so this could be an option for a design in its own right.

COLOURING

Everything I'd seen and read on the colouring stage suggests the use of 'archivist quality' permanent marker pens. These should minimize the bleeding on the wood and should be incredibly long lasting. However, I couldn't source them locally and, while there were some available online, I didn't have time to order them. An alternative option was to use wood stain. The range I used is spirit-based and colourfast so should work well, but I needed a really fine-bristled brush to reach right around the beads, and the only one I had was in a bit of a sorry state.

The supplier of the pyrography kit had included some Derwent Inktense water-soluble ink pencils, along with some 'water brushes'. These are plastic tubes filled with water and screwed to a tiny brush tip; by stroking the brush on the surface it gives a very controlled application of water. I could colour in the area using the ink pencil, then add water using the water brush. The water dissolves the coloured pigment on the wood and spreads it evenly like an ink. These pencils are a professional artist-grade product, giving a light-fast and chemically stable finish which can be applied to almost any surface, including wood and fabric, as well as more traditional painting surfaces.

I found the pencil a little soft for colouring wood so needed to sharpen it regularly to give the best access around the beads. It didn't really matter if I missed any parts as the water brush spreads the colour and with

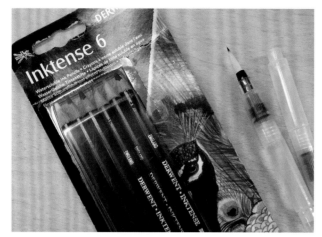

Inktense pencils and water brushes

Using the pencil

The first two repeats look promising

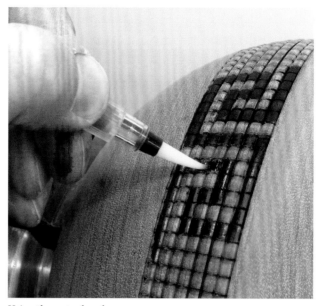

Using the water brush

The Greek key design complete

such a fine point gives great control. So often products that claim a lot don't deliver, but this really impressed me and painting the Greek key pattern into the appropriate squares was a very enjoyable experience.

My main area of concern as I painted – obviously being incredibly careful to stick to my pattern – was whether my maths was correct and that the pattern would meet up around the other side as it should. Thankfully everything worked out exactly as planned and I was over the moon with the result.

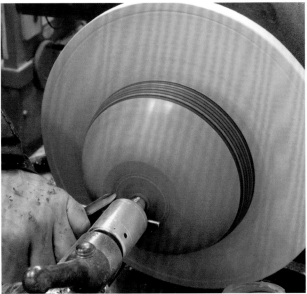

Finishing the bottom of the vase

Spray finishing with satin lacquer

FINISHING

The final job, once the colour was dry, was to mount the bowl between a disc of MDF mounted on a faceplate and live centre, and remove the chucking tenon. I then finished it by applying three coats of satin lacquer, lightly rubbing back between coats with a fine pad. I decided a spray-on finish would be best, avoiding the possibility of smudging the colour work.

CONCLUSION

Despite my early reservations about this project, I thoroughly enjoyed making it. The pyro work was rather tedious, but compared to those who really get into this technique, my little band of detail was a breeze, and an excellent way of trying the technique without spending days working on a piece. The end result is effective and actually better than I imagined it would look.

The finished piece

Seashell and resin inlay

My challenge to make a turning using resin inlay happened to coincide with a family holiday by the seaside. I am not an artistic turner, but I know plenty who are, and they all tell me that they draw inspiration from everything around them, whether from things in the natural environment or from textures and patterns that appear in architecture and the built environment. Inspired by the seashells on the beach, I tasked my sons with filling their buckets with seashells, and they didn't let me down. Back in the workshop with plenty of shells, I thought my mini texturing tool could be used to create extra effects. After a few experiments I found a setting that produced a swirling pattern that looked like a whirlpool. Perhaps if I combined it with some blue-tinted resin, I might be on to a winner.

RESEARCH ON RESIN

Having little experience of casting resin, I set about doing some online research. After reading about various products I stumbled across a company called Easy Composites, and a product called GlassCast 50 Epoxy Casting Resin. This product is primarily designed for producing things such as 'river tables', which involve natural edge boards of timber being fixed together with a coloured resin 'river' running between them. The description says it is suitable for castings up to 1in (25mm) thick in a single pour, and thicker by pouring more layers after a certain amount of time. Most importantly, it is 'water clear' and 'thoroughly de-gases itself during curing', which means that air bubbles shouldn't be an issue – I understand they often are when using resin. It seemed ideal so I ordered a 2lb (1kg) set, along with some tinting pigments for the pattern on the underside of my bowl.

I had a lot of shells to work with

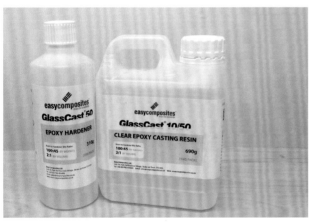
GlassCast 50 resin and hardener

DESIGN

I selected a board of walnut which was a good size for what I had in mind, around 9¾in (250mm) wide and 2in (50mm) thick. I drew circles on the board to give me an idea of the layout for the inlay. I selected a few small shells, averaging around 1⅛in (30mm) across, with the thickest being around ⅜in (9mm), so a groove around 1⅜in (35mm) wide fit the bill well.

My next decision was the layout of the shells. My natural inclination was to have things laid out in an orderly fashion, and I could have set them out giving a natural 'top' to the bowl, with all the shells upright. The other option was to lay them out radiating from the centre so there is no 'top' as such. I decided this worked best for me. Of course, they would also look good in a more random pattern as they would naturally be found on the seabed, even combined with sand and stones perhaps.

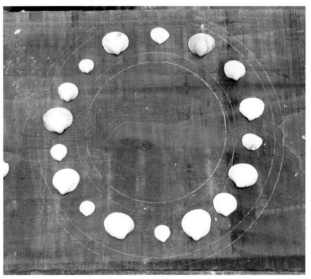
Experiments with the layout of the shells, giving a top to the bowl

Radiating from the centre

Adding texture to the foot

The finished texture, bordered with V-grooves

TEXTURE

I would have preferred to add the texture at a later stage, but the natural order of turning meant that had to be done quite early in the turning process. The blank was roughed and trued round, the chucking tenon turned and a foot initially cut. Then I was ready to add the texture. The texturing tool was easy to use with the 17-tooth wheel fitted and set on the second mark from horizontal, with the wheel running clockwise. I drew some lines on the foot to mark the area I wanted to texture and went for it. It was simply a case of lightly applying pressure to the wood with the tool's wheel until the desired texture was formed. In practice, I found too much pressure for too long led to very deep grooves with a quite regular spacing, but I wanted a more random spiral pattern, so less pressure for less time worked best. I'd recommend lots of experimentation to find the pattern that works best for your intended design.

Satisfied with the pattern, I used a point tool to cut grooves either side of the texture to frame it. My intention was to later pour tinted resin into this texture to achieve a whirlpool effect to tie in with the seaside theme of the bowl.

FINISHING THE UNDERSIDE

With the texture complete, I finished turning the underside into an ogee shape, which I felt worked well for this type of shallow bowl. As there would be a groove in the top to house the shells, the ogee needed to be a deeper shape than I would usually make. Happy with the shape and the foot (which was slightly larger than I would generally go for due to the whirlpool texture) I could sand the bowl, which was done by hand from 180 down to 400 grit.

CUTTING THE GROOVE

Holding the bowl by the tenon I trued up the top surface and marked out the position of the groove for the shells. I initially cut the groove with a spindle gouge, squaring it off with a negative rake scraper. The gouge cut on the vertical walls left a clean surface, whereas the scraper worked best for the flat bottom. With the thickest of my chosen shells being ⅜in (9mm), I wanted around ½in (12mm) for the groove to give a good covering of resin. As the groove got deeper I was acutely aware of the curve of the underside. The last thing I wanted to do was part off the rim, yet I was a little shy of the depth I needed. Looking at the shape

Cutting the bottom of the groove with a negative rake scraper

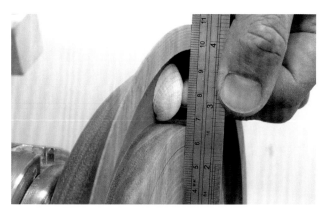
Testing the depth of the groove

of the shells gave me a solution. The thickest part of the shell will be towards the centre of the bowl, so a gradual slope to the floor of the groove would solve my issue well. Without making the outer part of the groove any deeper I formed a slope, testing it regularly with the largest shell and a ruler until I was satisfied with the depth.

WOOD MOVEMENT

Wood movement is always a potential issue, especially when dealing with a product such as epoxy, which is notoriously inflexible when cured. I decided to hollow the bowl out before pouring the resin. When making bowls with designs such as a painted rim, generally you apply the paint and then turn out the bowl afterwards to reveal the raw wood beneath the paint, but here this was less of a problem, as long as I aimed well with my resin pour. The issue was more of movement. As any woodturner knows, removing the centre of a bowl will release a lot of tension from a blank and the bowl will need to settle into its new shape, usually moving to some degree during and after the turning process. I thought it best to allow this to happen before the resin pour to minimize the possibility of issues at a later date. Ideally, I would turn it and leave it to one side for a few weeks before the resin pour, but, as always, time was against me, so after sanding to 400 grit I moved straight on to the pour.

MIXING THE RESIN

Epoxy resin is a two-part mixture of the resin itself and a chemical hardener. Everything I had read about using epoxy suggested that getting the volume of the mixture right is hugely important, so I used my digital scales to get the mix just right. The two bottles supplied a total of 2lb (1kg), but how much did I need? Thankfully the Easy Composites website has lots of information and a useful video on using the product. Working out how much to use was a simple sum: as directed by the video online, litres and kilograms should be considered the same (they aren't quite, but it's close enough for this). So I needed to multiply the length needed (the circumference of my groove) in metres, which was 0.644m, by the width of my groove in metres, 0.030m, by the depth of my groove in millimetres, 12mm, which gave an answer of 0.2318 litres; I was happy to call that 250g (0.25kg). The mix I needed was a ratio of 100:45 resin to hardener, so I poured 173g of resin and 77g of hardener into a clean mixing cup and thoroughly mixed them together.

Turning the inside of the bowl

The sanded bowl, ready to pour the resin

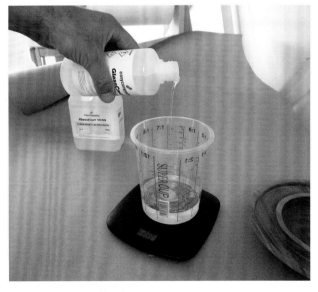
Mixing the resin and hardener

POURING AND LEVELLING

The bowl was sanded to 400 grit and I blew it down with my airline outside to remove any dust from the surface. I poured a small amount of the mixed resin into the groove. With this light covering I placed the shells on top. I considered gluing them down but didn't want this to show up later so I just placed them into the resin. Satisfied, I poured on the rest of the mix. There were little bubbles showing but they began to dissipate as I watched, so I hoped they would all disappear during the curing process.

As I poured to the top, I noticed that one side seemed higher than the other and realized my bench wasn't 100% level. While the resin was thicker than water, with a consistency more like a thick oil, it still self-levelled like any other liquid. I remedied this by folding a piece of paper and placing it under one side of the bowl.

Satisfied with the pour so far, I watched it for a few minutes, fascinated by the little bubbles slowly rising to the surface. To my horror one of the shells slowly rose to the surface too. The thought had crossed my mind, but after considering where shells are found (on the seabed and not floating in the sea) I thought seashells were not too buoyant. However, I hadn't accounted for air being trapped on the underside of the shells as I poured the resin. The shell floated up to the surface, a bubble popped out from beneath and, with a little help from my stirrer, I placed it back in position on the bottom of the groove. I continued to watch and, one by one, the shells each rose to the surface to let out their trapped air and I pushed them each back down into position.

WHIRLPOOL EFFECT

The next morning when I returned to the workshop I was pleased to see the shells where I'd left them. The resin had to be left for 48 hours to fully cure before it could be worked, but after around 16 hours it was hard enough to turn over so I could pour in the whirlpool inlay. I followed the same procedure as before, only this time guessing at the amount of the mixture I needed. Making the numbers easy, bearing in mind the weight ratio of 100:45, I poured 100g of resin and 45g of hardener. Once mixed together, I added just a few drops of blue pigment with the aim of making it look like a tropical ocean. The liquid easily poured into the textured area and now I just needed to wait. By the end of the day, the remaining mixture in the pot had thickened but was undoubtedly still liquid. The pour on the whirlpool had settled well into the texture but had levelled up to the chucking tenon, which I had hoped to avoid, but I would just have to deal with it once the resin was cured.

Placing the shells in a small amount of resin

Pouring on to the shells

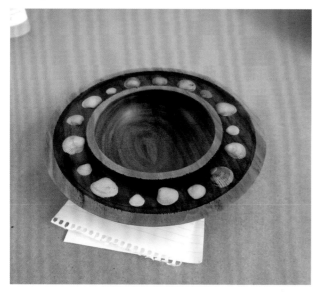

Allowing it to cure, levelled with a folded piece of paper

Adding the blue tint to the mix

Pouring into the texture

POURING AND TEST TURNING

Forty-eight hours after the whirlpool pour, it was all ready to take back to the lathe for finishing up. The main pour over the shells looked great. I could leave it at that or maybe tidy it up a little. There were just a couple of areas where the resin had seeped into the end grain of the bowl's rim. There was also an area where I had obviously turned a little too thin in the groove, and some resin had leaked through the pores of the wood and left a resin puddle on the outside of the bowl, but this

should hopefully sand away easily. The whirlpool on the underside certainly needed flattening and smoothing out as it was well proud of the wood, not to mention I needed access to the chucking tenon.

I looked at the remaining resin in the pot, which I had left to one side. The lollipop stick/stirrer was stuck fast in the cured resin and, with a little squeeze of the pot and a wiggle of the stick, I found that I was holding a block of cured resin on a stick. Immediately I knew that this was a

The cured whirlpool inlay

Some resin leaked through the bowl

The remaining resin is cured and useful to experiment with

Turning the cured resin

Turning the resin on the base

Sanding away the leak

Careful sanding of the rims

Removing the tenon

great opportunity to see how the resin would turn. I have turned various resin and plastic materials over the years – some are brittle and chip easily, some turn best with a negative rake scraper and are best not turned with conventional tools – so I was curious to experiment before going to work on my bowl.

I snapped off the lollipop stick and chiselled it flush so I couldn't catch myself on it, then mounted the disc of resin between centres. The first test was to try cutting with a spindle gouge. This would quickly tell me how easily it turns. I was amazed by the long streamers that came smoothly from the resin. After several enjoyable but messy passes with the gouge, I inspected the resin and was pleased to find a smooth surface that resembled frosted glass. A negative rake scraper gave equally good results. My next test was to try to sand and polish it back to the same level of clarity as it was before. Despite careful sanding to 1,200 grit, using burnishing cream and buffing with a mop loaded with a very fine white compound, which leaves most things positively gleaming, I couldn't return the resin to the full 'water clear' level that it was straight from the casting. This bothered me as I really didn't want to spoil the bowl as it looked so good.

TURNING THE BASE

I decided to finish the underside and ponder what to do with the top as I worked. I mounted my faceplate with a disc of MDF fixed to it, and sandwiched the bowl between it and the live centre, lining up with a centre mark I had previously made. Turning the underside went to plan: the resin turned away easily with a skew used as a scraper, although the long streamers were more than a little annoying and remarkably strong, and needed clearing regularly. As I'd hoped, the spot of resin that leaked through was easily removed with careful sanding.

I flipped the bowl and studied it again. I decided that I didn't want to spoil the clarity of the resin and so did not touch this again, other than carefully sanding the edges, which would hopefully remove any signs of the seepage into the end grain. Sanding from 240 to 400 grit did the trick and I decided to give it a wipe of oil to see if it would be visible after finishing. I was pleased that, as the walnut darkened under the oil, there was no visible trace of the seepage and the walnut itself showed some lovely figure, too.

Satisfied with the look of it, I remounted the faceplate and MDF disc and the bowl, once again bringing up

Close-up of the top detail

the live centre for support as I turned away the tenon. A little sanding smoothed the foot and when I took the bowl from the lathe the remaining pip was easily removed with a carving gouge and some gentle power and hand sanding. I oiled the bowl with three coats of satin hard wax oil to finish it.

CONCLUSION

I was really pleased with the outcome of this challenge, although if I were to do it again, I think it would be worth experimenting with using more shells, sand and stones to produce a more natural beachscape. I was impressed with the GlassCast 50 resin and I feel, with a bit more experience, I could easily produce even more impressive results. The whirlpool texture on the underside is OK – I think it does roughly what I intended and shows another use for the resin, although the tint would be more effective with some back lighting, maybe used like a stained-glass window.

I am always my own biggest critic but I think that's the best way to improve; be critical and learn from everything we do.

The finished whirlpool inlay

Brass wire inlay

When I was challenged to incorporate brass wire in a wooden turning, I wondered what would be best to make. I have seen people use wire to 'stitch' cracks in bowls, but cracked bowls aren't really my thing. I had never worked with brass wire before so I looked online for ideas. Scrolling through Instagram, I came across the work of Hyde & Gallagher, cabinetmakers based in the Cotswolds; they had made a range of furniture featuring accurate star charts laid out in brass. This got my brain ticking, especially as my oldest son is fascinated by space.

EXPERIMENTS WITH WIRE

I searched online and found a company that sells a mixed sample pack of 0.01in (0.4mm), 0.02in (0.6mm), 0.03in (0.8mm) and 0.05in (1.25mm) in rolls of 13–33ft (4–10m); I figured this would give me lots of scope to experiment. With the star chart idea still rumbling around in my head, I also ordered some short lengths of brass rod from eBay, 12in (300mm) lengths of 1/16in (2mm) and 1/8in (3mm). It's not technically wire, I know, but sometimes you have to just roll with an idea.

My first experiment was to create a band on a piece of spindle work. This must be the most basic way of using wire, but I thought it would be interesting to see just how easy it was to do. I turned a piece of walnut into a cylinder and cut a small groove around it using a point tool. I then cut a length of wire and experimented with getting it into the groove. My preference for sticking metal to wood is always a two-part epoxy resin, but this takes 30 minutes to set and I quickly discovered that the wire needs to be held in place while the adhesive cures, otherwise it wriggles away. It is tricky stuff to handle. I decided CA glue was going to be the way forward, even though I'm not a fan of it, and will avoid its use wherever possible. I find it tends to stick brilliantly when you don't want it to, and lets you down whenever you really need it to hold. In this case, however, it seemed to be the answer. I tried initially with just the glue, but even CA doesn't grab quick enough for my liking, so I tried it with some accelerator spray and this worked much better.

My first attempt was poor in every way – it was lumpy, uneven and generally a mess. My second attempt went much more smoothly. This time I ran the wire through my fingers, encouraging it to curl into a shape more to my liking and less like the tight, uncontrollable coil that it came in; this made it far more manageable as I lay it into the groove, adding CA and accelerator spray as I went. I snipped the end of the wire so that it sat snugly next to the other end in the groove and glued it down, holding it carefully in place with the tip of my awl.

I left this to dry thoroughly and placed a board of walnut into my vice to see how it worked on flat work. I decided the easiest way to cut a tiny groove would be with a carver's V-tool. I ran a couple of lines in the wood, one with the grain and one diagonally across it. The razor-sharp tool cut cleanly in the walnut in any direction, which was encouraging. I snipped off some pieces of wire and lay them into the grooves. They didn't lie particularly flat, having come from a coil, but with a little manipulation between my fingers, I managed to straighten them somewhat. I ran CA glue into the groove, laid the wire into it and sprayed accelerator. The accelerator produced a kind of bubble of glue over the wire, which I found interesting.

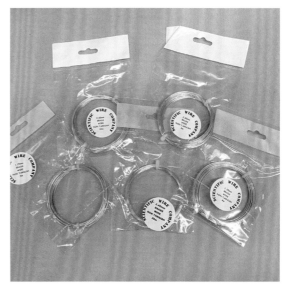
Selection of mixed wire

The first attempt wasn't good

Wires fitted to the flat board

Straightening the wire with my hammer

Turning the wire in the groove

The results are very promising

The test wires in place and sanded

EXPERIMENTAL CLEAN-UP

I left the glued wires for a couple of hours. I always try to leave adhesives longer than necessary to cure – nothing good ever comes of rushing glue. Looking at the wires on the flat board, I decided the easiest way to clean them would be with my belt sander, so I gave them a light buzz over and was pleased to see they looked almost as I'd hoped. They needed more though, so I sanded again. The next time I looked, the wire running in line with the grain was gone. I believe the combination of heat and the aggressive nature of the tool caused the glue to let go. The wire running diagonally survived better but it clearly hadn't been lying entirely flat in the groove as it appeared as a variable thickness line. I needed to straighten the wire better before putting it into the grooves.

After a bit of thought, I cut a length of wire and laid it on the board of walnut. I drew the face of my hammer repeatedly over the wire, rotating it regularly until it was almost completely straight. I was sure this would make things easier, so I cut a couple more grooves in the walnut and glued in pieces of the straightened wire.

While this dried, I headed over to the lathe and had a go at cleaning down the wire wrapped around the walnut cylinder. This time, rather than sanding, I used a negative rake scraper to lightly scrape off the glue and true up the brass. I started with my second attempt as I was not hopeful that the first would stand up to much. I was very pleased with the result. A clean line of brass shined as it reflected the light from my lamp; even the join in the wire was quite neat.

I returned to the flat piece and, knowing that the belt sander was too aggressive, this time I tried my orbital sander and the result was much better. I could feel a slight difference in the surface as the sander removed more wood than brass, leaving it slightly uneven, but still acceptable.

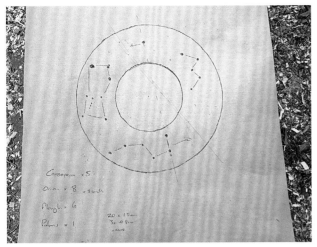
My initial drawing of the 'constellation bowl'

Belt sanding isn't the way forward but I have 'proof of concept'

DESIGN

The more I thought about it, the more I liked the idea of a 'constellation bowl' with stars, linked by wire to show some of the best-known constellations. I checked through my woodpile and found a board of 9in (230mm)-wide, 1½in (40mm)-thick walnut, which would be perfect. Walnut would be the ideal partner for the brass. I thought a wide-rimmed bowl would work best, so I drew it out full size on craft paper to plot out my constellations.

The three most prominent constellations in the night sky above me here in the UK are Orion, Cassiopeia and the Plough, which is part of Ursa Major, or the Great Bear, and famously points to Polaris or the North Star, so I decided to add this too.

On my drawing, I placed Polaris at the top, with the Plough at the bottom, pointing to it. On either side, I placed Orion and Cassiopeia. I drew it out a few times before I was happy with the positioning. I thought the

⅛in (3mm) brass rod would represent the stars well. There are, of course, other stars in the sky, so I decided to randomly add smaller stars in the open spaces, using the 0.05in (1.25mm) wire. I experimented by fixing each size into the walnut board and sanding them down flush. As before, the belt sander was too aggressive and the heat build-up was too much, but if cleaned up more gently I was certain this would work.

THE BOWL

I cut a disc from the walnut board and mounted it on the lathe. Generally, I would turn the underside first into a sweeping ogee shape, but, in this case, I needed to work on the top face and it needed to sit flat on the bench without wobbling around while I did so.

To achieve this, I initially sandwiched the blank between the chuck and my live centre and cut a holding tenon with my narrow parting tool. I then flipped it over and worked

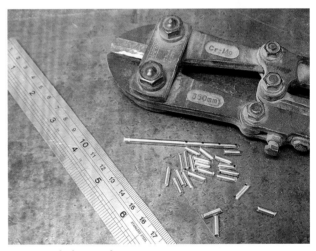
Preparing the brass rod

Marking the positions of the stars with my awl

Drilling for the brass rods

Tapping the brass rods into place

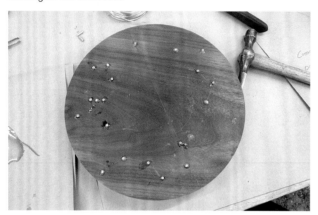
Left aside to dry, but looking good

Turning the brass rods

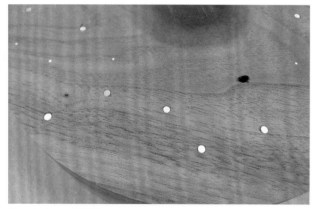
One star went AWOL

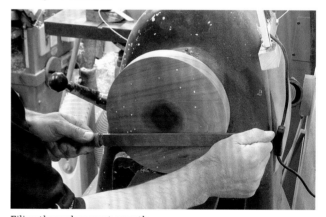
Filing the replacement smooth

the top face, holding it securely in the chuck. I would turn the underside afterwards.

I turned a very slight curve into the face of the bowl, gave it a light sand with 120 grit and sealed it with sanding sealer. In my experiments, I hadn't had any issue with contamination between the brass and the wood, but I figured it never hurts to give it a little more protection.

I cut the ⅛in (3mm) brass rod into ⅜in (10mm) lengths using bolt croppers. I needed 20 for my planned layout.

Orion also has three smaller stars which form a sword, hanging from the three stars that make up his belt; I decided to show these with three 0.05in (1.25mm) wire dots. I set out the constellations on the rim of the bowl, adjusting a couple of times until I was entirely satisfied. I then marked the position of each star with my awl to ease the drilling. I took it to my drill press and drilled ⁵⁄₁₆in (8mm) deep holes with a ⅛in (3mm) drill, followed by ¹⁄₃₂in (1mm) holes for Orion's sword and a random selection of holes in the open areas, which I had marked out by eye.

THE STARS

With the holes drilled and the wire and rods cut, I mixed up some epoxy. The CA glue would work for the wires, but I thought epoxy would give a much more secure fixing for the stars. I quickly found that my fingers were too big to easily hold the short pieces of brass, even using my small pin hammer, so I grabbed a pair of tweezers from my first-aid box. Usually used for removing splinters, they worked almost as well for holding the brass rods as I tapped them into place. I left them overnight to fully cure.

After giving it some thought, I decided the easiest way to remove the excess brass sticking out of the bowl was going to be to turn it. I remounted the bowl and sharpened my ½in (12mm) bowl gouge (⅝in/16mm bar). I turned the lathe gradually up to 1850rpm. I believe brass should turn better at high speeds. I used the wing of the gouge in a gentle draw cut across the face of the bowl and stopped it to check. Some of the brass rods showed a clean, shiny end, which proved it had worked, so I carried on turning it until I made some fine wood shavings and once again stopped the lathe. It had worked well, except for one star from the Plough which had gone AWOL. I didn't see, hear or feel it go, but it had slightly enlarged the hole, so I would have to replace it and fill around it with some dark filler-wax. I replaced the missing rod and, after leaving it for a couple of hours, returned it to the lathe. This time I didn't turn it as it was likely to pull out again, so I filed it smooth by hand. I power sanded the whole thing with 120 grit to ensure it was smooth and even, ready to cut the grooves for the wire.

JOINING THE DOTS

I began by drawing a line with a sharp pencil and steel ruler, between the stars of each constellation. I decided the spacing between the stars of Orion's belt and sword was too close for the wire links, so didn't add them there. With it all drawn out I began cutting the lines. As I had in the practice piece, I used a razor-sharp V-tool.

I carefully sliced a shallow groove along each of the lines, trying my best to ensure an even depth all the way along and on each line. The thin curls that the tool produced were incredibly satisfying, and it didn't take me long to cut all of the lines.

Next I needed to add short pieces of wire into each of the grooves. I cut a piece of 0.03in (0.8mm) wire around 12in (300mm) and, as before, used the face of my hammer to rub part of it flat and straight. It wasn't perfect, but would hopefully do the job. I marked the length of the first piece

Literally joining the dots

Carving the grooves with my V-tool

Snipping the wire to length

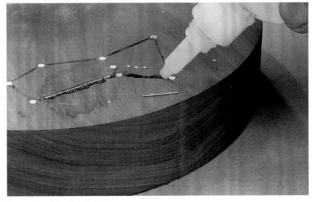

Running CA glue into the groove

I needed and snipped it off. A test fit looked promising so I ran some CA glue into the groove and pushed the wire into the bottom of it with the tip of a pencil and my awl. Satisfied it was lying as flat as possible, I sprayed accelerator to set it in place. I repeated this process on each groove until each constellation was marked out.

The bowl was a bit of a lumpy, gluey mess but showed signs of looking how I imagined it. I left it overnight to fully cure and returned to clean it down the next morning.

Removing excess with my orbital sander and 120 grit

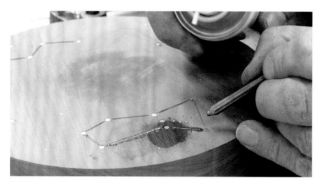
Adding accelerator

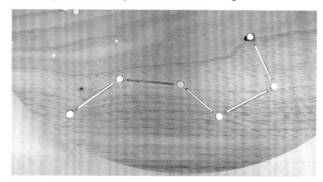
Another piece is missing

Orion is ready to clean down

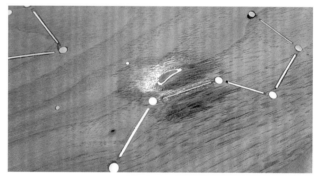
The replacement glued in place

SANDING

Initially, I used my orbital sander with 120-grit abrasive to remove the excess glue and smooth the surface. I then remounted the bowl in the lathe and sanded through to 400 grit using abrasive wrapped around a cork block. I decided this was the most gentle and controllable way of smoothing everything out without wearing away the wood more than the brass. In between each grit I stopped the lathe to check my progress. Each time the brass was a little more sparkly, but as I checked it after the 320 grit I spotted a casualty. One of the wires in the panhandle of the Plough had vanished!

I returned the bowl to my bench and cut a new piece of wire. Using the V-tool, I cleared out the dry glue from

Final sanding on the lathe

Turning the inside of the bowl

Turning the underside of the bowl

the empty groove and then, using a ¹⁄₃₂in (1mm) drill bit, I scraped at it a little more until I was happy that the new piece of wire would sit neatly. I added a bead of glue, carefully placed the wire and added some accelerator. As before, I left it for an hour or so to cure. I needed to take great care here not to disturb any of the other wires which were sitting shining at me so perfectly, but I needed to remove the excess glue.

After giving it some thought I decided to continue to use my orbital sander. By approaching from the centre of the bowl I shouldn't touch the other wires too much, and by using just the edge of the pad I could target the problem area. This is technically bad practice as it can produce a hollow in what should be a flat surface, but with care, I managed to get the result I wanted. I then sanded as before, using the cork block, through to 400 grit and this time everything stayed where it should.

FINISHING
I was very pleased with the look of the constellations. All I needed to do now was hollow the bowl, finish the underside and add a few coats of oil.

Using the tip of my skew in scraping mode, I scored a mark where I thought the bowl should go. After checking, I enlarged it slightly and began to hollow. I made the bowl

slightly undercut to add interest and shadow. Once I was happy with the depth and curve, I sanded to the same 400 grit as the rest of the bowl.

I use a disc of MDF, which is permanently fitted to a faceplate, to re-turn the bases of bowls and I did the same here, only it was the entire underside of the bowl that needed turning and not just the chucking tenon. I turned a shallow, sweeping ogee shape and sanded this to 400 grit as well. The remaining small pip where the live centre was pinching it to the MDF disc was easily carved away with a carving gouge and power sanded smooth.

I used a dark wax filler stick to tidy the slightly enlarged hole around the star in the Plough that went AWOL and applied the first of four coats of my favourite hard wax oil. Finally, I buffed it with my dome buffing brush.

CONCLUSION
To me, this challenge showed the joy of the creative side of woodturning – you just never quite know where it will lead you. Despite my strong dislike of CA glue and the loss of a couple of pieces during the turning, I felt the project went well. The combination of walnut and brass is always a winner for me, the effect of the constellations looks great and the grain that has appeared within the hollowed bowl adds to the night sky effect of the piece.

Oiling the bowl really sets off the brass against the walnut

The finished bowl

Pewter rim bowl

The first time I saw pewter on a turning was on a quaich, made by well-known pole-lathe turner Robin Wood in his book, *The Wooden Bowl*. I have since seen pewter used by well-known turners such as Simon Hope and Stuart Mortimer, and I was eager to try working with it myself in this project. Pewter is a soft metal that lends itself to use by turners as it has a relatively low melting point of between 338–446°F (170–230°C) depending on the exact mix of component metals, which means it is easily melted over a domestic stove without the need for industrial equipment. Being quite soft, it will turn with standard high-speed steel (HSS) turning tools, making it ideal to add to turned work as a feature.

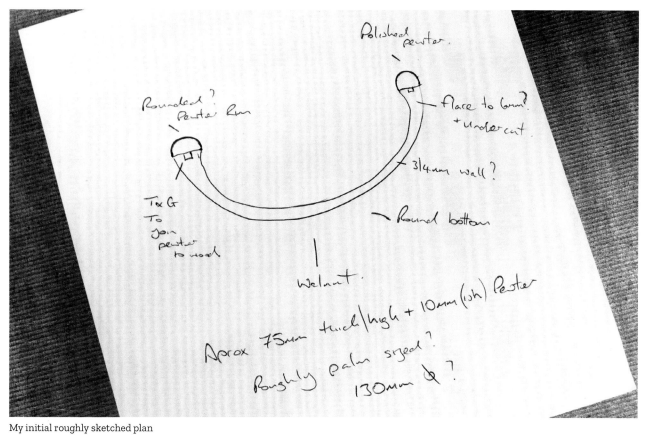

My initial roughly sketched plan

QUAICH

Taking my inspiration from Robin Wood's turned quaich, I decided to turn a small bowl with a decorative pewter rim. A quaich is a traditional Scottish drinking bowl with carved handles, often associated with whiskey. As a nod to these early drinking bowls, I planned to make a palm-sized, round-bottomed bowl, but for purely decorative purposes and without the carved handles.

THE THEORY

My knowledge of working pewter was entirely based on what I had seen in a number of demonstrations over the years and having read a few articles in magazines and on the internet. It seems quite straightforward as pewter will melt in a pan over a stove and can be cast into a simple wooden former or mould. If this went to plan, I would fix the cast pewter ring to the rim of a bowl and turn it all together into a finished decorative bowl. It should be reasonably simple, although I expected a few challenges along the way.

TIMBER SELECTION

Pewter, once polished, has a shiny silver appearance, so I thought a darker timber would suit this job best. To me, the addition of a polished pewter rim suggests a luxury, high-end product, so my choice of timber was an easy one. Walnut is one of the most expensive commercial hardwoods, although not considered exotic. It's a deep chocolate brown colour that would contrast well with the polished metal and the two materials should work beautifully together. The plan was for a palm-sized bowl, roughly 5¼in (135mm) in diameter. I had some 3in (75mm)-thick American black walnut in stock, which fitted the bill perfectly.

DESIGN

I always make some sort of plan; sometimes I write it down or make a sketch and sometimes it stays in my head. In this case I sketched out my idea with a few notes to make sure what was rattling around my head was actually going to work.

I needed a good way of attaching the pewter to the bowl, so by forming a kind of tongue and groove joint between the two, I thought I should have a good surface area to allow epoxy resin to bond them together.

TURNING THE OUTSIDE OF THE BOWL

I'm sure this could be done in a number of ways and the various steps could be done in a different order, but to me at least, the order I worked in seemed logical. My first step was to turn the outside shape of the bowl. With this turned, I would know exactly what I was going to be working with, which would hopefully eliminate some guesswork.

The outside shape was a simple curve, I just needed to leave enough additional timber on the base to be able to achieve a continuation of this curve at the end, while leaving myself a good chucking tenon to grip the bowl. Happy with the curve, I sanded the outer surface, for no other reason than it seemed like a good idea.

The next step was to prepare the rim to accept the pewter casting. My intention was to cut a groove in the rim of the bowl with my thin $\frac{1}{16}$in (2mm) parting tool and to cast the pewter with a corresponding tongue, which should give me a good strong join. I turned the rim of the bowl around $\frac{5}{16}$in (8mm) wide, double checking it was dead flat with a steel ruler, then cut a $\frac{1}{16}$in (2mm)-wide groove in the centre, approximately $\frac{1}{8}$in (4mm)

deep. I also made a couple of cuts into the bowl just to distinguish the rim, but left the bulk in the centre of the bowl, hoping this would keep the bowl stable while I sorted out the pewter.

THE MOULD

At this point, there wasn't much more I could do to the bowl itself until I had cast the pewter ring, so my next job was to make a mould/former in which to pour the molten pewter. There were a number of choices available to me here: I could use an offcut of timber but it would need to be dry timber as any moisture present in the wood could react with the molten pewter and cause it to spit back dramatically (and dangerously!) as it was poured. Timber can also be prone to movement, which could also cause headaches further into the process. I had seen MDF used in demos; this has the advantage of being stable, unlike solid timber. As I expected the boiling pewter to burn the mould somewhat, I didn't really want to have to deal with MDF smoke as well as everything else that was likely to be happening during the pour.

I settled on using good-quality birch ply, which seemed to be the best of both worlds having great stability, but being

The bowl is turned and the next stage is casting the pewter

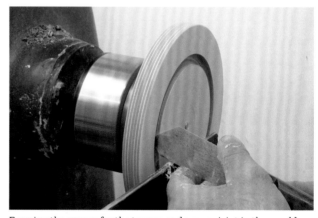

Forming the groove for the tongue and groove joint in the mould

The rim of the bowl and the mould ready for the next stage

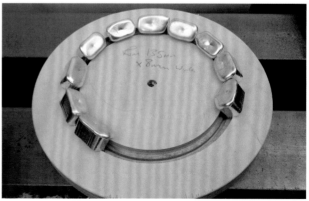

The mould with the pewter ingots

less noxious than MDF. I also had several suitable offcuts in the workshop which were crying out to be used.

I carefully measured the rim of the walnut bowl and transferred the dimensions to the ply, which I cut into a disc and mounted on a screw chuck on the lathe. Erring on the safe side, I cut the groove in my former around ³⁄₈in (10mm) wide with a ¼in (6mm) beading and parting tool used as a scraper, giving me ¹⁄₃₂in (1mm) extra of pewter on each side of the rim. I expected a little shrinkage in the pewter as it cooled so I guessed this would be fine. With the groove for the pewter cut around ⁵⁄₁₆in (8mm) deep, I then cut a narrow groove with my ¹⁄₁₆in (2mm) parting tool, which would form the tongue in the pewter. Again, in case of any shrinkage, I cut this groove around ¹⁄₈in (3mm) wide, which should also allow a little for fitting it into the groove in the bowl. Sitting the bowl upside down on the former, it all seemed to fit together well, which was encouraging.

PREPARING THE PEWTER

I ordered some lead-free pewter online, in 1oz (28g) ingot form; this was not the most economical way to buy it but I needed it quickly. I bought my pewter from an eBay seller, which was easy to find and organize. I have since found it at a much better prices elsewhere online. If you want to use pewter, another option is to repurpose old pewter from things like beer tankards, which are often available in charity shops. The only issue with recycling old pewter is that it is very difficult to know if it contains lead, which is of course hazardous to health. If you choose this route extra care and personal protection must be taken, in particular the use of breathing protection during the melting process.

I wasn't sure how much I would need so I ordered 10 pewter ingots. Having cut the channel in my plywood mould, I laid my 10 ingots in the groove to see if there would be enough metal. Not being terribly mathematically minded, but having a reasonably good eye for quantities, I estimated that, as my channel isn't as wide or deep as the ingots, the fact that there is only enough ingots to go three quarters of the way round the former shouldn't be an issue and I probably had just about enough. I'm sure it would be possible to work out things like the volume of the ingots and that of the channel but to be honest, I just wanted to get to the melting part, so that's what I did.

Having bought a small gas camping stove and a pan from local shops, I set the stove and pan up on the loading bay outside of my workshop. While this was essentially

going to be like cooking soup or perhaps gravy over my hob at home, I was really not comfortable doing that in a workshop filled with wood, sawdust, wood shavings and flammable finishes. While it would certainly be possible to give the workshop a thorough deep clean and tidy an area to work in, I didn't have the several weeks to do this just now, not to mention that my insurance provider would not be at all happy with me burning an open gas flame in the workshop. All in all, outside on the loading bay seemed like the most sensible option.

I set up a plywood screen to shelter my working area from wind and laid out everything I needed, close to hand. My loading bay is a useful working height and I often use it for glue-ups and other jobs that require more space than is available inside the workshop. I wore my long-sleeved turning smock, a full face shield and some protective gloves, just in case. While the process seemed to be a simple case of boiling a pan over a stove, I thought it best to proceed cautiously.

THE CASTING

With everything set out on the loading bay I was ready to make a start. I turned on the gas with the pewter ingots in the pan and it took what seemed like an age before anything happened. I gave them an occasional stir, more for something to do with my hands than for any real reason, I think. Gradually the ingots began to melt. As the metal became soft, the amount of liquid increased and the ingots became like melting ice cubes in a pool of quicksilver, until the pan just had liquid pewter swilling around inside.

Once I was sure all of the metal had melted, I was ready to pour it into the mould. I had looked for a pan with a spout – I think they are known as milk pans – but could only find a standard pan, which I hoped

The pewter ingots are melting well

would be fine. Straightaway I missed the groove and ended up with a puddle of pewter on the rim of the mould, but I quickly improved my aim and was able to run it round the channel. I was surprised how quickly it hardened off and how high it sat above the ply of the mould. There was nothing else I could do now the mould was full. I had assumed I would need to leave it overnight to cool and fully harden, but it quickly became apparent that as soon as everything had cooled to a normal temperature I would be able to remove the casting from the mould.

Pouring the pewter

The cooled and cast pewter stands well proud of the mould

It looks like the cooled pewter has shrunk slightly in the mould

HEALTH AND SAFETY

As ever, health and safety is largely common sense. Melting the pewter should be done away from anything combustible, so ideally outside in a sheltered area – it is highly unlikely your insurance would cover you should anything go wrong in the workshop. Personal protective equipment should be worn throughout including gloves, long sleeves and a face shield as a minimum. Breathing protection is certainly advised if there is any possibility of lead being present in the pewter.

REMOVING THE PEWTER FROM THE MOULD

I had assumed that as the pewter cooled it would shrink a little in the mould, making it easy to separate the two. I was wrong! Despite it looking like it had shrunk slightly, it certainly did not release itself from the mould; if anything it had welded itself to it. Initially, I tried prying and levering it with screwdrivers, knocking and banging it on the concrete floor and even cutting away excess plywood on the bandsaw, all to no avail. The only option left was to turn away the ply former to release the pewter ring. I was slightly apprehensive doing this but it was the only way to separate the two parts. I remounted the mould on the screw chuck and carefully turned away the plywood. My biggest fear was the pewter ring would I suddenly come away and become an airborne hazard, but this didn't happen. In fact it clung to the mould even after there appeared to be no contact between the two materials.

Throughout, I regularly stopped the lathe to check the contact between the two and eventually I managed to prise them apart. This was far more difficult than I had expected – perhaps ply isn't the best material or perhaps I should have better prepared the mould. This is an area I will need to experiment with to find the best solution.

WORKING THE PEWTER

The pewter, now free of the mould, was reassuringly solid and weighty, but with a very rough and uneven surface. I would need to clean it up to fit it to the bowl, so I fit my wooden plate jaws to my chuck and turned a shape that would hold the pewter ring in expansion mode. The tongue on the pewter was rough and oversized, as planned, so my next job was to trim it down and fit it to the bowl. I took careful measurements from the groove in the bowl and used my negative rake scraper, which is a repurposed round skew, ground straight across to gently reshape the tongue. I was pleasantly surprised by how easy pewter was to work. With the scraper, I largely got dust rather than long shavings, but the surface revealed

Turning the pewter from the ply mould

Finally free of the mould

by the tool was clean and shiny. After several passes and trial fits I was satisfied with how the two parts fitted together and was ready to join them.

I have always found epoxy resin to be an excellent way of fixing wood to metal, so didn't hesitate to use it here. I mixed the two parts of the resin and spread it around the rim of the bowl and into the groove, fitting them together, then left them to one side to cure overnight under some heavy weights. Despite my care in applying the epoxy, I still managed to dribble some down the side of the walnut bowl. Luckily, I had fine sanded the outside of the bowl so this minimized any marking or staining from this.

TURNING THE BOWL

With the epoxy fully dried, I could get on with the turning the next morning. I once again used my scraper to tidy the pewter and bring it level with the walnut, before switching to my bowl gouge and making a shearing cut over the wood and the pewter to ensure a flowing curve. Interestingly, the gouge produced some longer shavings from the pewter. Happy with the outside I rounded over the top of the pewter rim with my scraper. You can see from the pictures how the dust came away from the rim,

which quickly went from square to round. Once I was happy with the rim, I continued to hollow out the rest of the bowl. This was just standard bowl turning, but with the added advantage of having the pewter rim to rest the bevel of my bowl gouge on as it entered the bowl, completely removing the chance of a catch on the rim of the bowl.

I was looking for a reasonably thin bowl so I regularly checked the wall thickness with my callipers. When I was happy with the turning, I could begin sanding, initially under power and then by hand. My biggest concern with sanding was that the pewter dust may contaminate and discolour the timber. To minimize the chance of this I tried to sand from the wood outwards toward the rim, sanding the pewter last at each grit and carefully checking the line between the two regularly. I took the whole thing to 600 grit and the pewter rim onward to 1,200 grit, finishing it very carefully with burnishing cream, which left it beautifully smooth and shiny.

I decided to place a very fine V-cut between the wood and pewter with my point tool, which made the joint as tidy as possible while also helping to disguise any

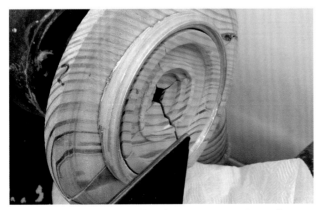
Pewter ring held with my wooden plate jaws in expansion mode

Beginning to shape the tongue on the pewter

Test fitting the bowl to the pewter rim

Carefully spreading the epoxy around the rim of the bowl

The following morning the epoxy is dry including the dribble down the edge of the bowl

Tidying the rim with my scraper

Cleaning the bowl and blending with the rim with my bowl gouge in shear cutting mode

Shaping the pewter with my scraper – notice the metallic dust from the tool

The rim, straight from the tool

subsequent movement in the wood. Finally, I reversed the bowl in my usual way, between a disc of MDF fixed to a faceplate and the live tail centre, removed the holding spigot and rounded off the bottom of the bowl. I removed the tiny pip that remained with a sharp carving gouge, power sander and then hand sanding.

CONCLUSION

I thoroughly enjoyed making this project and, overall, it was a success. The bowl has a lovely shape, sits nicely in the hand and rocks pleasingly when nudged on a flat surface. The contrast between the pewter and the walnut worked just as well as I had hoped, both materials complementing each other perfectly.

After making this first experimental bowl I was commissioned to make a set of bog oak bowls with pewter rims for a client and so was able to refine the process considerably from that shown in the original magazine article. I realized that the way the pewter stuck to the mould could be used to my advantage. Rather than trying to cast the tenon/tongue onto the pewter, I simply cast it in a deeper channel than I needed and turned the tenon into the cooled pewter with the mould mounted on the screw chuck on which it was originally turned. This saved several steps and once I test fitted it on the bowls, I could turn it free from the mould and it was ready to epoxy straight onto the bowl, rather than needing to remount and rework it.

The pewter I had used for the article wasn't particularly good quality – note my mention of producing dust as I scraped it. The better-quality pewter that I now use turns in long streamers and generally works far more easily than the ingots I bought for the article.

I have since developed casting and working pewter into a demo that I have toured around turning clubs in the UK and it is always well received. I would cast into solid wood for this without a problem but would always emphasize that it should be fully seasoned, dry wood and not green, as this would be dangerous.

Turning the inside of the bowl

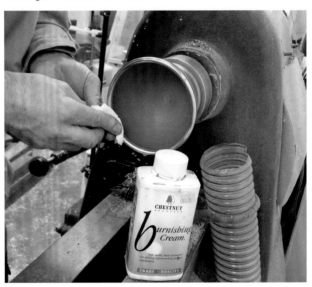
Burnishing the pewter – very carefully – to a high shine

Adding the tiny V-cut between the walnut and pewter

Compass inlay platter

When I was challenged to turn something with a wooden inlay pattern, I immediately knew what I wanted to make: a bowl with an inlaid design made from different timbers in the centre. By coincidence, I had recently been admiring the turning work of a friend on Instagram. Paul Jasper (@copper_pig_fine_woodworking) makes all sorts of geometric inlays which look like stylized stars and flowers, using assorted woods and even some metals. I had never done this kind of work before and didn't really know how it's done, but I was keen to find out.

RESEARCH

I didn't want to directly copy Paul's work, but he was the obvious person to turn to for advice about the methods involved. He explained that they are actually quite simple and it is just a case of cutting a series of small, accurate triangles, then sticking them together. He uses a tablesaw jig to produce his little triangles; the blade on mine doesn't tilt so this could be a problem for me depending on the design I chose.

I did some internet searches for inlay and veneer patterns and one jumped out at me straight away, the design known as a nautical star or a compass rose. Its history is as a decorative detail on ships' compasses. I found a very informative video on YouTube which showed a method of making them with a simple bandsaw jig. The video (www.youtube.com/watch?v=BNqIXp2rnPQ) showed a couple of different versions, but I decided to go with the most simple of the designs shown for my first attempt.

Triangles are 35mm wide
8mm high
22.5° angle
Approx. 20mm sides

16 pieces
8 x walnut
8 x maple

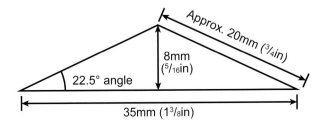

DESIGN

I decided to use a maple and walnut combination for my compass star. The video showed me how to cut the pieces and that they needed to be triangles with angles of 22.5°/135°/22.5°. What I didn't know was how big each of the little triangles needed to be. The only way I could work this out was to produce a full-sized drawing of my design.

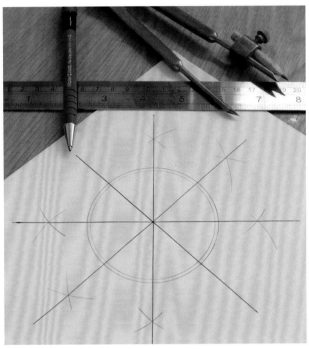

Beginning to lay out the design

TIMBER AND LAYOUT

Searching through my timber pile I found a lovely piece of 2in (50mm)-thick quartersawn European oak of around 11in (280mm) diameter, which would make a perfect small, shallow bowl or platter for me to inlay the star into. I drew a few circles on the blank to determine that a star of around 2¾in (70mm) point to point should work well. If I could inlay the star into another contrasting piece of timber and turn this into a disc, it would be quite easy to set that into the base of my oak platter.

I began by drawing a 2¾in (70mm) circle on paper with a compass and drew a vertical line through the centre. With this baseline drawn it was then just a case of bisecting it several times. This was done by setting the compass to an arbitrary distance somewhat wider than the radius of the circle. With the point set at the 12 o'clock point where the baseline crosses the circle, I drew an arc outside the circle at the 3 and 9 o'clock areas. I repeated this with the point set at the 6 o'clock point where the baseline crosses the circle. These sets of arcs form crosses outside the circle at the 3 and 9 o'clock positions. By lining up the centre of the crosses and the centre point of the circle with a ruler, the line I drew was exactly at 90° to the baseline.

I repeated this bisecting process eight times, until I had 16 evenly spaced lines radiating out from the centre of my 2¾in (70mm) circle. By drawing a second circle, half the diameter of the first, using the same centre point I could now plot my triangles. Starting with the line immediately to the left of the 12 o'clock, I followed it from the centre point to the first circle, then joined it back to the 12 o'clock line at the point it meets the outer circle. This was the first of the little triangles. To complete the layout, I repeated this process, shading every other one with pencil to represent the darker-coloured wood.

I could now take the measurements from this carefully drawn layout: the little triangles needed to be 1⅜in (35mm) along the long face, ⁵⁄₁₆in (8mm) tall with the other faces being ¾in (20mm). I also knew that I needed to cut eight in each timber.

BANDSAW JIG

I decided a simple sled that sits over my bandsaw table would be the easiest jig to make and operate. I found an offcut of MDF a little longer than the table of the saw and, with the MDF clamped to the bed, square to the blade, I glued and screwed softwood battens to the overhanging sides of the MDF, placed tightly to the side of the table. Once fixed in place I removed the clamps and tested the sled to ensure it moved smoothly, adding a little candle wax to the underside and the battens.

I generally use a ⅜in (10mm) wide, 6tpi blade in my bandsaw as I find it is the most versatile option, allowing the saw to be used for most cutting operations that I need. For this project, however, I ordered a wider ½in (12mm) blade with a finer 10tpi. This should produce straighter cuts and leave a finer surface, meaning I should need less sanding to fit the little triangles together.

With the new blade fitted, I made a cut into the base board of the sled. This gave me a baseline from which to measure my 22.5° angle needed to cut the triangles. I used my digital protractor to position a batten and screw it to the base board as a fence. I then made a few test cuts, positioning a stop block on the fence in the correct position to produce the triangles of the perfect size I need.

TIMBER PREPARATION

Knowing the sizes of timber I needed made it a simple job to rip strips of maple and walnut to the required sizes. The thickness of the wood I prepared would be the depth of the star I made, so I went with long pieces of 1⅜in (35mm) wide and ⁵⁄₁₆in (8mm) thick, all cut with the fine-tooth blade on my tablesaw. This left a surface good enough for this job, as each would be further cut and sanded.

The first cut on the end of the timber produced one of the faces of the triangle. By turning it over and placing it against the stop block, the next cut produced the other face of the triangle, with the base of the triangle against the fence. It was a quick job to produce the 16 little triangles that I needed and I was very pleased with the accuracy from the saw. I laid the pieces on my drawing to check how well it was all working so far.

The bandsaw sled in use

Cutting the little triangles

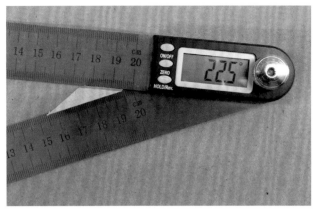
Checking the angles

Laying the triangles on the drawing

GLUE-UP

As usual when gluing up, I placed a large piece of brown craft paper on my bench to keep it glue free. I wrapped a sheet of 180-grit abrasive tightly around a board of MDF; I lightly rubbed the long faces of the triangles against this to make them smooth and flat. I then spread a thin layer of glue over this face and rub-jointed it to the long face of another triangle, pairing the maple and walnut together to form little monochrome diamonds. Carefully lining the triangles up and holding each together for a few moments while the glue grabbed, I then set them aside to dry while I paired the rest of the pieces.

Forming walnut and maple diamonds

Set aside to dry

Sanding the diamonds ready for the next phase of the glue-up

Gluing the diamonds together

The two halves ready for fitting together

Sanding the halves until the fit is perfect

Glued up with elastic bands

When the glue was dry, I carefully sanded the four faces of the little diamonds to remove the bandsaw marks and laid them out in the right order before I started gluing them together. I alternated maple and walnut, carefully lining up the diamonds which now formed something resembling the petals of a flower.

As I knew from my experience of previous segmenting projects, the chances of forming a complete and perfect star straight from the saw were pretty remote, so I glued up the two halves of the star separately, but allowed the glue to dry before moving on to put it together entirely.

The halves matched well, but not perfectly, so once they were dry enough to handle, I flattened the faces which would be glued together on the abrasive block. I tested a few times and adjusted until I was satisfied and then made the final glue-up. This time, just to give a little more evenly spread pressure, I wrapped the star in a couple of elastic bands while it dried fully.

SLICING THE STAR

Satisfied that the glue in the star was suitably dry, I flattened both faces to better see the joints. I was very pleased with the outcome. I now needed to slice this into a thinner piece that I could inlay. At 1³⁄₈in (35mm) thick I should be able to make a few, as I calculated that ¼in (6mm) would be plenty to let into the bottom of my small platter. Obviously cutting the star on the bandsaw in its current state was not an option from a safety point of view, so I glued it to a planed offcut of timber that I had in my timber pile and clamped it while it was drying. The video I had watched suggested using double-sided tape for this, but I preferred the more secure glue option.

Once dry, I set up a fence on the bandsaw and took a test cut, producing a thin veneer; I was pleased to see just how solid it was. Happy with this, I made another cut, producing a ¼in (6mm)-thick nautical star that I could use for the project.

I could just fit this into the platter but access would be fiddly to say the least, so I decided to inlay the star into a piece of sapele, hoping the red of this wood would frame and set off the star. I prepared an oversized block of sapele and gently clamped the star to it, lightly marking it and the sapele with an X so I could place it back in exactly the same position. I used a sharp chip-carving knife, which works very well as a marking knife, to mark the outline of the star. This technique is used

Faces of the star sanded

Fixed to a piece of wood ready to slice on the bandsaw

Test cut of a thin veneer is promising

Using a knife to 'draw' around the star

Ready to glue in

Beginning to chop out the star

Using a cabinet scraper to clean down the star

So far, so good

Turning the inlay into a 3in (75mm) disc

Inlay block ready for slicing

Turning the inside of the platter

extensively in fine woodworking as a knife cut and, done well, is far more accurate than a pencil line.

From here, I could cut in on the knife line with a sharp chisel and mallet and then begin removing the centre. This process is a little like fitting a hinge when hanging a door, albeit an incredibly awkwardly shaped hinge. After an enjoyable 40 minutes of chiselling and paring, test fitting and a little more paring, I was satisfied enough to glue the star in place. I liberally spread glue into the star-shaped recess and carefully tapped the star into place with a scrap block and mallet. I then used a cabinet scraper to smooth out the surface.

Next, I cut the sapele into a disc on the bandsaw and mounted it on my lathe, carefully lining up my live centre with the centre of the star, and carefully turned it to 3in (75mm) diameter, which framed the star beautifully. I was very hopeful that once oil was applied to this it would really pop.

The sapele I had inlaid the star into was over-thick and needed cutting down, so I used the same approach as before and glued it to a larger block, allowing me to safely push it through the bandsaw to produce the ¼in (6mm)-thick disc ready to be fitted into the platter.

TURNING THE PLATTER

The quartersawn oak blank had some lovely ray flecks, characteristic of this cut of oak. I mounted it on a screw chuck and turned the underside into a sweeping ogee shape, which is a favourite of mine for the underside of platters and shallow bowls. I predominantly use a ⅜in (10mm) bowl gouge (½in/12mm bar), shaping the curve and finishing with a shearing cut before sanding through to 400-grit abrasive.

Turning the platter over and holding it on a tenon, I was able to turn a narrow curving rim with a small step detail, before turning a slight undercut and curving down into the platter. Bearing in mind that I would be letting in a ¼in (6mm)-thick disc into the platter, I left it a little thicker than I perhaps normally would, focusing instead on producing a pleasing curve.

I set a pair of dividers to the diameter of my inlay and marked the position. I then used a ½in (12mm) round skew, ground straight across as a negative rake scraper, and cut the recess to take the inlay. I regularly checked the fit of the disc and, once I was satisfied, took the depth down to a point where the inlay sat just proud of the oak.

I spread a liberal coat of glue around the recess and, carefully lining up the grain direction of the insert with the platter, positioned the inlay, bringing up the tailstock, fitted with a wooden block and applying light pressure to the inlay. I left it to dry overnight.

FINISHING

The next morning I was pleased with how the inlay looked in the platter. It was standing a couple of millimetres proud of the oak so my next job was to blend it in. With a freshly sharpened gouge I took a few light passes, checking the finish regularly. I really didn't want to tear the star detail at this point. Despite the intricate details of the design, at the point it meets the edge of the gouge, it was all face grain, so it cut very smoothly, although the star noticeably resisted the cut less than the oak. This meant I had to be careful to keep the cut as smooth as possible without accidentally removing more wood from the inlay.

Satisfied with the finish from the tool, I began sanding. There were a couple of tiny gaps between the star and the sapele border so I applied some hard wax oil and began sanding. As I hoped, the slurry produced by this 'wet sanding' technique filled the tiny gaps and as I sanded through the grits to 400, I was pleased with how it looked. I reversed the platter on my MDF disc fixed to a faceplate, sandwiching it with the live centre, and turned away the chucking tenon. I preferred to use a ⅜in (10mm) spindle gouge for this as I found it better suited to working in the tight space close to the live centre. The tiny nub that was left was pared away and power sanded with 400 grit to blend it with the rest of the foot.

I finished the platter with three coats of hard wax oil, which brought out the colours of the inlay beautifully.

CONCLUSION

I thoroughly enjoyed making this project. The combination of turning and the other bench skills involved really ticked the boxes for me with work I enjoy most. I would usually expect something with this level of 'wow factor' to take a lot more work, but actually the inlay was really quite simple to make. Of course, there is room for improvement – next time I would try to avoid the little gaps that showed between the star and the sapele border. Overall though, I am pleased with the combination of timbers I chose, the shape of the platter and the look of the inlay.

The inlay glued in place and left to dry overnight with light pressure

Cleaning down the inlay

Reversing the platter to remove the tenon

Oiling the platter

Resources

SUPPLIERS

Crown Tools: Turning tools
www.crownhandtools.ltd.uk

Axminster Tools: Chucks and drive centres
www.axminstertools.com

Woodart Products: Pyrography machine & Inktense crayons
www.woodart-products.co.uk

Chestnut Products: Finishes
chestnutproducts.co.uk

Treatex: Hard wax oil
www.treatex.co.uk

RECOMMENDED READING

Woodturning Projects: A Workshop Guide to Shapes by **Mark Baker**
GMC Publications, 2003

Woodturning: A Foundation Course by **Keith Rowley**
GMC Publications, 2015

The Wooden Bowl by **Robin Wood**
Stobart Davies, 2009

About the author

Richard Findley is a full-time production turner based in Leicestershire in the UK. His background is in woodworking, having trained as a joiner and worked in the family joinery business. He comes from a long line of woodworkers going back at least five generations. It is the variety of work that he enjoys, undertaking commissions for one-off prototypes to large production runs, turning for furniture makers, restorers, architects, designers and joiners.

His work is mainly based in the UK, but his growing reputation for making the highest quality turned work has earned him commissions for items that have gone to the US, Canada and Australia.

Richard is a well known and popular demonstrator and has travelled widely around the UK, Ireland and the US. He has written for *Woodturning* magazine since 2010 and has a strong following on Instagram.

Email: richard@turnersworkshop.co.uk
Website: www.turnersworkshop.co.uk
Instagram: richard_findley

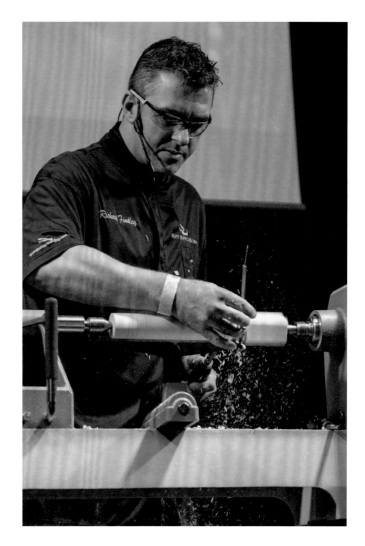

ACKNOWLEDGEMENTS

To my wife Vanessa for her support and patience over the years and for my sons William and Oliver who might enjoy reading this one day.

Photograph by Nathan Savory

TURNING DECORATIVE BOWLS

First published 2023 by
Guild of Master Craftsman Publications Ltd
Castle Place, 166 High Street, Lewes,
East Sussex BN7 1XU

Text © Richard Findley, 2023
Copyright in the Work © GMC Publications Ltd, 2023

ISBN 978-1-78494-673-9

Publisher Jonathan Bailey
Production Manager Jim Bulley
Project Editor Karen Scott
Managing Art Editor Robin Shields
Designer Jonathan Bacon
Photographer Richard Findley

Colour origination by GMC Reprographics
Printed and bound in China

To place an order, contact:
GMC Publications Ltd
Castle Place, 166 High Street,
Lewes, East Sussex,
BN7 1XU
United Kingdom
Tel: +44 (0)1273 488005

www.gmcbooks.com